AGAMEMNON'S CROWN

By the same authors
The Golden Apples of Hesperides
(The Book Guild, 1999)

*For Julie
For Happy Mornings.
by Audrey Knight*

AGAMEMNON'S CROWN

William and Audrey Knight

The Book Guild Ltd
Sussex, England

First published in Great Britain in 2001 by
The Book Guild Ltd,
25 High Street,
Lewes, East Sussex
BN7 2LU

Copyright © William and Audrey Knight 2001

The right of William and Audrey Knight to be identified as the authors of this work has been asserted by them in accordance with the Copyright, Designs and Patents Act 1988.

All rights reserved. No part of this publication may be reproduced, transmitted, or stored in a retrieval system, in any form or by any means, without permission in writing from the publisher, nor be otherwise circulated in any form of binding or cover other than that in which it is published and without a similar condition being imposed on the subsequent purchaser.

Typesetting in Times by
IML Typographers, Birkenhead, Merseyside

Printed in Great Britain by
Antony Rowe Ltd, Chippenham, Wiltshire

A catalogue record for this book is
available from The British Library

ISBN 1 85776 504 4

CONTENTS

THE PRECEDENT	1
THE UNIFICATION	35
HED'S TALE	87

ACKNOWLEDGEMENT

Our thanks go to Ashley Price, without whose splendid work typing up the plays, these books would never have happened. Generous thanks are also due to the loving and caring staff of Osborne House Convalescent Home, Isle of Wight, for inspiration.

William and Audrey Knight

INTRODUCTION

In *The Golden Apples of Hesperides,* the first play, called *Seek the Fair Helen*, is set at the time of the destruction of Troy.

The first two plays in *Agamemnon's Crown* deal with the following period, leading up to the second play in *The Golden Apples of Hesperides* about Tisamenes.

Everyone knows the stories about Agamemnon and Menelaus, Helen and Paris, Achilles and Hector and, though they belong to a land distant in time and space, we look on them as our own.

Most of us can find something to say about the next generation, Electra, Iphigenia, Hermione, Pyrrhus and Orestes. But who of us, apart from scholars, can even name the next generation – Tisamenes, grandson of Menelaus; Pergamus, grandson of Achilles? The names mean nothing to us. And not even the scholars can say how Cometes, son of Tisamenes, fared after his escape, or name his children.

For those people were almost obliterated in the Dorian invasion and little comes through to us. Orestes ruled firmly till his death at a ripe old age; Tisamenes lasted only three years – betrayed by Philomenus, they say – and was chased northwards to Helike; Cometes got away to the islands. The decipherment of Linear B tablets tells us fragments of what happened at Pylos when the Dorians came.

Then we start picking up the Dorian lineages; the names of the men who took over the Achaean citadels; men like Aristodemos, Temenus, Chresphontes, and Aletes, Lord of Sicyon.

But how did he get there? Aletes is not a Dorian name – it is a name from an earlier Royal House; not the Achaean Dynasty, of

Agamemnon and Orestes, but the earlier one which started with Andromeda. For Aletes descends from Clytaemnestra and Aegisthus.

Well, there ought to be a story in this – and this is our version. If it does not match up with your own picture of these times, all we can say is that Professor Blegan's excavations and Ventri's translations indicate a way of life somewhat different from that described by Homer.

Two minor points: firstly, in these plays we use the 'Minyan' not in its strict ethnic sense but as a general term of derogation for all the peoples conquered by the Achaeans; secondly, Tyrcenus is the only person you won't find in the histories of that time; of course there must have been an Achaean Lord of Sicyon before Aletes, someone whose name is lost to us, and Tyrcenus 'of the strong walls' is as good a name as any.

William and Audrey Knight

THE PRECEDENT

INTRODUCTION

A fine chariot is drawn up at the water's edge, and as the ship comes alongside she is boarded by three men from the chariot. They salute Agamemnon, and after a few quiet words from the leader of the three, Agamemnon, elated, turns to the man at his elbow, gives a few brief instructions and leaves the ship accompanied by the three from the chariot.

As general disembarkation from the ship begins, Agamemnon climbs into the chariot and sets off on the journey which will end with the embrace of Mother Labrys; the journey which began on the day Troy was fired.

On that day, in the throne room of Mycenae, the Queen, accompanied by her councillors and Aegisthus the King, are Tyndareus (father of the Queen) and Perilaus (cousin of the Queen) attending to the petitions of her subjects.

All the proceedings take place in the shadow cast by the silver sacrificial axe hidden behind its curtain high above the back of the throne.

CHARACTERS

Queen Clytaemnestra   *Mother on Earth*
Aegisthus   *Husband of the Queen*
Electra   *Daughter of the Queen*
Tyndareus   *Father of the Queen*
Perilaus   *Cousin of the Queen*
Steward

PLACE

The Throne Room in Mycenae.

In the throne room of Queen Clytaemnestra.
TYNDAREUS   Your words are law; we will act on them.
AEGISTHUS   Hurrah! Another precedent!
CLYTAEMNESTRA   And the next for my attention?
TYNDAREUS   A petition, if it please you, Lady.
AEGISTHUS   Proceed!
CLYTAEMNESTRA   From?
TYNDAREUS   From Aloxitas, a plough-wright, born in
    Sicyon, where he still lives.
CLYTAEMNESTRA   Proceed, my father!
TYNDAREUS   His wife, Aethra, having turned him out of
    house,
  Has taken to her bed one of the Corinth messengers . . .
AEGISTHUS   For shame!
TYNDAREUS   Therefore he humbly begs that, at your Royal
    command,
  The messenger be whipped and he, the plough-wright re-
    instated.
  For he cannot ply his trade without his tools,
  They being in the workshop next the house.
AEGISTHUS   Do not apportion blame between the woman and
    the messenger,
  Whatever punishment is laid upon the messenger, put also
    on the wife,
  Even a whipping.
PERILAUS   Steward! More wine for Lord Aegisthus.
CLYTAEMNESTRA   But surely he may take his tools away.
  They are not detaining them?
TYNDAREUS   No, my Lady. Indeed, the answer by the
    woman, Aethra,
  Is that the tools and timber be removed at once;
  Dilapidations put to rights; the ground outside made clear.
CLYTAEMNESTRA   Then why . . . ? He can build another
    workshop somewhere else.
  This is pointless . . .
  Born in Sicyon, you say. Of northern parentage, I would
    suspect.
TYNDAREUS   Second generation immigrant, my Lady.

CLYTAEMNESTRA   This is quite infuriating.
   They know the customs of my kingdom
   Yet still they act as if they lived beyond the Corinth wall.
PERILAUS   If I may raise a secondary point,
   May we be assured the Corinth messenger has not become
     neglectful of his job?
STEWARD   I can speak for him, Lord Perilaus.
   He is an able man, well-thought-of in the service of the
     Queen.
AEGISTHUS   He sows where poor Aloxitas has ploughed.
CLYTAEMNESTRA   Not suited, I think, my Councillors?
TYNDAREUS   Agreed.
PERILAUS   Agreed.
CLYTAEMNESTRA   The usual formula.
TYNDAREUS ⎱
PERILAUS   ⎰   Your words are law; we will act on them.
CLYTAEMNESTRA   And the next for my attention.
TYNDAREUS   Corinth again, my Lady.
CLYTAEMNESTRA   Proceed, my father.
TYNDAREUS   My Lady, this started as a routine application at
   the wall
   By a team of migrant workers, men of all tribes...
AEGISTHUS   Men of none!
TYNDAREUS   For entrance for the harvesting.
   Their leader, Cleodaeus...
AEGISTHUS   Ah, son of Hyllus, I should think.
TYNDAREUS   ... claimed he had a contract in Kynuria,
   But the man he named died many months ago, gored by a
     bull –
   You may have heard of it.
AEGISTHUS   Statius of Kynuria, blind in one eye; a widower.
TYNDAREUS   His successor, though willing to employ the
   migrants
   Concedes he has no contract, nor can he from his own
     experience
   Or knowledge, vouch for the applicants.
CLYTAEMNESTRA   How many?
TYNDAREUS   Fifty, my Lady.

AEGISTHUS   Are their women with them, and their families,
     Or do they come alone?
CLYTAEMNESTRA   Is not that rather a lot to harvest one
     small-holding in Kynuria?
AEGISTHUS   Perilaus, defender of the realm, what do you say?
PERILAUS   Steward, more wine for Lord Aegisthus.
TYNDAREUS   Their leader says the fields are steeply pitched
     And men tire quickly on the slope.
AEGISTHUS   Bosh! Not if they cut towards the rise. It's easier.
TYNDAREUS   The present owner used to farm along the
     coast
     And is not certain what his current labour force should be.
CLYTAEMNESTRA   Bind them in the Mother's name to be of
     good behaviour
     And to leave upon the winter's rains. Agreed?
TYNDAREUS ⎫
PERILAUS ⎬ Agreed!
AEGISTHUS   In the Mother's name? The Pamphilloi?
     Upon the name of Heracles would be a better oath.
TYNDAREUS   Madam, do you think...
     We are not proceeding very fast, and interruptions do not
     help.
CLYTAEMNESTRA   My dear, do you think you might...
     inspect the guard?
PERILAUS   Eh?
CLYTAEMNESTRA   Hush, cousin.
AEGISTHUS   Thank you, my Lady. I think I have had wine
     enough
     To imitate dear Perilaus on his daily rounds.
     Perhaps a change of disposition for the troops
     A strong detachment for Kynuria... (AEGISTHUS *exits*)
PERILAUS   My Lady...
CLYTAEMNESTRA   Hush, we can call them back again.
     His time is nearly up; it would unsettle anyone.
     Now, where were we...?
TYNDAREUS   Your words are law; we will act on them.
CLYTAEMNESTRA   Oh, it's agreed, is it?
     And the next for my attention.

PERILAUS   You know, my Lord Tyndareus, if these migrants at
    the wall
    In fact are nothing more than cattle thieves
    It is a bit remiss of Attica to pass them through.
TYNDAREUS   We have decided otherwise, my friend.
    I do agree, however, that Attica is not particular
    As to the persons she permits to cross her boundaries.
    There have been many instances ... (*to*
      CLYTAEMNESTRA)
    For example, in your mother's time, my brother had to call
      an army up to clear the land ...
CLYTAEMNESTRA   He was killed in the fighting, was he not?
TYNDAREUS   Indeed, he was, unfortunately.
    And Attica, all bland and hypocritical, denied all knowledge
    Of the passage of what must have been an army through
      their land.
    Spontaneous rising by disaffected teams of workers they
      opined!
    Denied they offered shelter to the beaten remnants, too!
    Supplicants from all nations come to Mother Attica! Indeed!
    We complained to Knossos, of course, but they had troubles
      of their own.
CLYTAEMNESTRA   What would be our course of action now?
TYNDAREUS   A direct warning, an ultimatum.
PERILAUS   War?
CLYTAEMNESTRA   No, not war!
TYNDAREUS   Not war on Attica! for, despite her perfidies
    She too gives honour to the Mother.
CLYTAEMNESTRA   Like us, her people are of the soil.
    Not conquerors, not immigrants, but since misty Time
    First let the days escape, we and they have shared this land.
PERILAUS   Cousin, am I the Leader of the Men
    The wielder of the sword that guards this land
    Or am I just a show piece like Aegisthus?
CLYTAEMNESTRA   You must not speak like that.
    War is for barbarians, and should they come once more to
      Corinth
    You wield the sword that guards this land.

TYNDAREUS   My Lady, my idle reminiscence led us to this argument.
Forgive me, Perilaus, I should have held my tongue.
CLYTAEMNESTRA   Let us get on.
And the next for my attention.
TYNDAREUS   An appeal from Argos, against a judgement by their Queen Hermione.
CLYTAEMNESTRA   Ah, my sister's child. Was her judgement sound?
TYNDAREUS   Mmm, well, hardly. Practical but not legal, one might say.
PERILAUS   Ha, that is where my military law scores over yours!
What is practical is legal, uncle.
CLYTAEMNESTRA   The facts.
TYNDAREUS   A farmer, having lost his wife ...
Well, he took his spears aboard a ship to Tenedos ...
CLYTAEMNESTRA   He serves that pirate, Menelaus.
TYNDAREUS   Indeed. No word has come for several years; he may be dead.
His son now is of age, and claims the right to sell off river pasture
To buy a vineyard on the hill.
There also is a daughter, not yet of age, but set on keeping
All the pasture land, there to breed horses.
CLYTAEMNESTRA   The decision?
TYNDAREUS   For the son.
CLYTAEMNESTRA   Absolutely?
TYNDAREUS   Absolutely. In effect it is decided that the father's still alive and still entitled to the farm.
The son as bailiff may do anything he likes.
CLYTAEMNESTRA   The man's an outlaw; it was as if he died the day he left the realm.
The daughter has a right to her inheritance.
TYNDAREUS   But being under-age, her brother ...
PERILAUS   As bailiff may do anything he likes!
CLYTAEMNESTRA   I see the way the mind of young Hermione works!

    She has more feeling for her father than she should in her
        position,
    And does not like to dub him outlaw, or his men.
STEWARD   My Lady, if I may ...
    I speak with diffidence, not having verified the facts,
    But there has been talk of more men leaving Argos for the
        East.
    Not random passengers, but ... well-organised.
TYNDAREUS   Interesting, but not quite relevant to the appeal
        in hand.
CLYTAEMNESTRA   Appeal upheld, I think, the son being
        accountable to his sister when of age.
TYNDAREUS ⎫
PERILAUS   ⎬ Agreed!
TYNDAREUS   Your words are law; we will act on them.
CLYTAEMNESTRA   And the next for my attention.
TYNDAREUS   Well, there is ... someone who claims to be a
        public supplicant.
CLYTAEMNESTRA   Is there any doubt?
TYNDAREUS   The procedure has been followed, but ...
    My Lady, it is your daughter, Electra.
CLYTAEMNESTRA   Silly child, as if we did not have enough
        to do!
    She can come and see me privately; there is no reason why
    Your time should also be drawn out unnecessarily.
TYNDAREUS   The procedure has been followed, Lady; you
        are bound ...
CLYTAEMNESTRA   But what's the point.
PERILAUS   Private disagreements thus are written down,
        becoming precedents.
CLYTAEMNESTRA   Oh, show her in, the ninny.
(STEWARD *exits and eventually returns with* ELECTRA.)
CLYTAEMNESTRA   What is it, child?
ELECTRA   Queen Clytaemnestra, Mother on Earth, I give you
        greetings!
CLYTAEMNESTRA   Yes, yes.
ELECTRA   From your humble subject, one Electra, born in
        Mycenae ...

(CLYTAEMNESTRA *looks to* TYNDAREUS, *who shrugs.*)
TYNDAREUS   It is the formula.
ELECTRA   A second generation immigrant ...
CLYTAEMNESTRA   Insolent child; your line runs through the centuries, unbroken.
ELECTRA   I am a northerner; by my father's blood I count.
CLYTAEMNESTRA (*grimly*)   Go on.
ELECTRA   Queen Clytaemnestra, I speak for ... many men. Every ninth year in this land ...
CLYTAEMNESTRA   This is no concern of yours!
ELECTRA (*kneeling*)   Hear my prayer, O Queen!
(CLYTAEMNESTRA *looks to* TYNDAREUS *again, who shrugs.*)
CLYTAEMNESTRA   Your prayer falls on my ear. Proceed.
ELECTRA   Many of your subjects, knowing that in this present year
   The ... old ... king goes his way, a new one comes,
   Would recommend to you a new king for your bed.
   A mighty man of valour, well endowed with untold gold.
TYNDAREUS   One moment, child.
ELECTRA   Grandfather Tyndareus, please let me finish.
TYNDAREUS   There is no precedent.
ELECTRA   Oh! Let us make precedents. Let us choose our king.
PERILAUS   Why should one look for valour in a king?
ELECTRA   Should not a king defend his realm, leading his fighting men?
PERILAUS   Hey ho! A farmer's life for me!
TYNDAREUS   Electra, child, these are the precedents:
   For the Queen's Councillors to note all likely princes
   From those countries whose customs are as ours.
   For the Queen's Councillors ...
ELECTRA   I should have known.
(*to* CLYTAEMNESTRA)   Queen Clytaemnestra,
   We would recommend to you ...
CLYTAEMNESTRA   Wait!
   If your petition is that a certain candidate should be added to the list,

This no doubt can be arranged, but would you first confirm
He is as Lord Tyndareus relates;
A conformer to the customs and religion of this land.
ELECTRA   We talk of kings, not shadows, and kings make customs.
CLYTAEMNESTRA   Not suited!
TYNDAREUS   Agreed!
PERILAUS   Agreed!
ELECTRA   Wait! Wait!
TYNDAREUS   Your words are law. We will act on them.
ELECTRA   This king will not wait on precedents but from his own mouth utter laws.
CLYTAEMNESTRA   Steward, remove the supplicant.
ELECTRA   This king will sit upon that throne ...
(*Exit* ELECTRA *screaming* 'This king ...'.)
CLYTAEMNESTRA   Never to enter this room again.
Disgusting exhibition! A child of mine!
She has too much time and would be better occupied
In bringing children to this world.
PERILAUS   My Lady, does she speak the truth?
CLYTAEMNESTRA   I beg your pardon?
PERILAUS   Is there indeed a candidate with popular support?
TYNDAREUS   Not that I have heard about.
CLYTAEMNESTRA   Anyway, she talks of a northerner, for sure.
A mountaineer in skins she would put into my bed.
TYNDAREUS   A prince beyond the Corinth wall?
PERILAUS   But not of Attica!
TYNDAREUS   No, not of Attica. There the Goddess reigns.
CLYTAEMNESTRA   But none, not even out of Attica, would have a following this side of the wall.
PERILAUS   The migrant workers! The Pamphilloi!
TYNDAREUS   A Dorian prince! Assassara me, deliver us from that.
CLYTAEMNESTRA   And what is a child of mine doing to be identified
With peasants and migrant labour teams?
Mad!

TYNDAREUS   Now that the subject has been broached, my Lady,
  It is the ninth year, after all.
  How does it go?
  'To keep intact the line that started with Andromeda
  Let the Queen bear children …'
CLYTAEMNESTRA   Seven have I borne and six of those still live!
  Is that not enough to keep intact the line that started with Andromeda?
  Five living daughters – is there not a queen you fancy in them all?
  Oh yes, I know the rules and precedents, yet every time I bring a daughter to this world
  I relegate the one before to a life-time in obscurity.
  Are they too young to know? Or does each, in turn, despair to see her mother thick with child
  Praying maybe to some dark god that it shall be a boy.
  Is that the way to raise a family in harmony?
  Look at Electra, my eldest. Four times superceded,
  How sour and truculent has she become!
  Chrysothemis jealous of her cousin, Iphigenia distant, Erigone silent.
  Now you bid me to a course of action which will cast a blight upon my youngest,
  Touch her eyes with shadows, still her tongue.
  How should I make her Queen-to-be?
  The alternatives; that I myself should die
  Or else Aegisthus by my hand. A bitter choosing that would be
  To one who would bring peace within her house.
  As you will! When the year is out and Aegisthus goes his way
  Bring a new king to my bed and I will do my best to bear him sons!
  Seven children have I borne, six still are left, but, oh, the one that died,
  My first-born, not just a Princess but for an hour or so the Queen-to-be

    For her father stood and died and proved himself a man.
    Is that your rule of law, my councillors, that you can take
        from me a man like Tantalus
    And in his place put – Agamemnon, slayer of my firstborn
        child.
PERILAUS   Cousin, I was eight years old! What blame on me!
TYNDAREUS   None. If blame there was it falls on me.
    The Achaean clan were useful allies when we fought the
        migrant folk
    But when my brother, Leader of the Men, died in the savage
        fighting at the wall
    An Achaean urged our spearmen on, and won a massive
        victory,
    Was then and there elected Leader of the Men,
    His sons ...
CLYTAEMNESTRA   His sons then claimed me and my sister
        as their spoils in war, and you permitted it.
    We were but children yet you permitted it.
TYNDAREUS   I said there was no precedent; that Tantalus had
        seven more years to serve
    But what were precedents to those well armed men.
    Why, Perilaus, you yourself remarked a little while ago:
    In military law, what's practical is legal.
CLYTAEMNESTRA   What of my daughter, what of my baby
        girl?
TYNDAREUS   I have no answer, child. It was wrong.
    It was wrong by any count, by any law. It was wrong.
PERILAUS   Why did you not call the people out
    And sweep the house of Atreus out of this land.
TYNDAREUS   One, it would not have brought the baby back to
        life.
    Two, to come between the army and the Leader of men is
        treason –
    You yourself know that –
PERILAUS   Hmm; in circumstances such as those ...
TYNDAREUS   Three, the migrant folk still skulked in Attica.
    It was not until that threat had disappeared
    That we dared ...

CLYTAEMNESTRA   We! *I* dared call the people out
    When Agamemnon sought to be a king perpetually.
PERILAUS   Hardly necessary this time, Lady.
    I hold the army to your service, though a one-armed man
        with a stick could see Aegisthus off.
CLYTAEMNESTRA   Do not speak of him like that, Lord
        Perilaus!
    He has behaved impeccably throughout his term of office
    And there will be no brawling when he has to go.
PERILAUS   Will he choose exile or the axe?
TYNDAREUS   Oh come, no-one has chosen the axe for
        centuries.
    Well not since my mother's time.
PERILAUS   But if he chose the axe?
CLYTAEMNESTRA   That is the law and I will act on it.
    You will excuse me if I leave you now; I find this
        conversation hardly to my taste.
    There is no further business left to do?
TYNDAREUS   No, my Lady.
PERILAUS   No, my Lady.
CLYTAEMNESTRA   Let my words be written down and acted
    on.
TYNDAREUS ⎱ Your words are law; we will act on them.
PERILAUS   ⎰
(*They bow.* CLYTAEMNESTRA *exits.*)
PERILAUS   And what would you have done, Tyndareus,
    If things had turned out otherwise?
    Because you had no sisters, the Queenship leapt your
        generation
    And settled on your child; but just suppose ...
TYNDAREUS   You mean if I had been the consort, and my
        wife the Queen?
    What choice would I have made?
    It is not easy, not having faced the shadow of the axe
    To give an honest answer.
    If I say I would have stood and died, there is no test which,
        when applied,
    Would show the truth of such an utterance, or serve to tell

    Whether I spoke bravely, knowing my death to be fair
        payment for a bargain I had freely made;
    Or whether being old, had not the wit to run away.
    Even if I say I would have run, is it because
    I now have proof that I had twenty further years to live?
    No, Perilaus, I can give you no answer that I know you
        would believe.
PERILAUS   Then, dear uncle, give me one knowing I will not
    believe it.
TYNDAREUS   This is my land; the hills that gave me birth
    May take my body back again.
    I do not wish my body laid at rest in alien soil
    By men who do not know my ancestry,
    Who do not care whether I came from Lacaedemon
    To save my life, or dodge a pressing creditor.
PERILAUS   You would have stayed, my Lord Tyndareus.
TYNDAREUS   When the shadow of the axe moves on, the
    scenery looks different.
    Who knows? The choice I might have pondered then might
        well be one Aegisthus ponders now.
(AEGISTHUS *enters unobserved*)
PERILAUS   And that?
TYNDAREUS   North for Locris, south for Crete?
(PERILAUS *and* TYNDAREUS *exit laughing*)
AEGISTHUS   North for Locris, South for Crete!
    Nine years I had, and they are nearly done.
    Nine years of – not power, no, that I never had –
    Of luxury, magnificence, the outer trappings of a king
    Yet not the king. I am the husband of the Queen;
    But what of that? I was not her first nor yet, I fear, her last
    And even 'husband' is too large a word to hang around my
        neck.
    I come when called – ha, yes – the phrase is doubly apt,
    I come when called.
    Thus stands the moon at certain times of year
    And then she calls 'Aegisthus, come to bed',
    And to the sound of trumpets and with a garland round my
        head

In procession I am led to her.
The outcome of this pleasant interlude is royal, is princely.
It was of course a lapse of taste, quite vulgar, to give her first
    a son
But I have atoned for it, not once but twice, with
Princess Elena, Queen-to-be, and young Erigone
The virgin priestess of the Moon.
Royal, divine; and even Prince Aletes will stand as Leader
    of the Men.
How magnificent the product of my seed! (*laughs*)
But if I put a farm wench on her back,
As many as I like,
And fill the countryside with daughters – what are they?
Common bastards, every one.
Nine years I had and they are nearly done
And every ninth year in this town they sacrifice the man
Who can with pride and dignity hold up his head and say
'I am the King.'
But if he can't, he runs away, just like my predecessor did
And shame and ignominy is his lot; his name despised.
Nine years I had – and do I run or die?

(*bitterly*)   O, Clytaemnestra, you who will not let me be a man,
    I will not run and be despised by such as you.
        Bring out your silver axe; here stands a man.
(*Enter* ELECTRA)
ELECTRA   Hail, great King, mighty monarch, fouler of my
    father's bed.
AEGISTHUS   And hail to you, sweet princess, dearest child.
ELECTRA   I am no child of yours, for Agamemnon is my sire.
AEGISTHUS   Agamemnon? I think I know the name. Now let
    me see ...
    Ah yes, the man who had no stomach for the lawful fate of
        kings
    But ran away. Did I say man?
    Well, as near to man as you are near to Queen.
ELECTRA   If they must spill my father's blood to make me Queen
    Then I would rather live a peasant's life!

AEGISTHUS   Spill his blood! No, there was little chance of that.
   He ran too fast.
ELECTRA   He did not run, you foul-mouthed effigy!
   There was work for men to do at Troy, while only weaklings stayed at home.
   Where were you when the call went forth to rescue Helen from her paramour?
AEGISTHUS   I think I fell asleep while waiting, child.
   When Helen left these shores, I seized my sword
   Eager to stand by Menelaus and see the insult to his honour cleared.
   But no call came. A year went by, two years, three.
   Seven years went by before the ardent Menelaus found he had no wife within his bed
   And raised the cry of 'vengeance'.
   Seven years before his brother Agamemnon offered aid!
   Tell me, child, was it just coincidence that at that time
   Their term of kingship came unto an end?
   They had the choice: to run or die. You know the rest.
ELECTRA   It was not so, adulterer! The oracle was cloudy.
   They had to wait until the omens were propitious.
AEGISTHUS   The omen of the axe was clear enough.
ELECTRA   They were not cowards, nor was any man
   Who went to face the might of Troy.
AEGISTHUS   You make it sound a brave adventure,
   Mighty heroes gathered, full of resolution
   To set their spears against the milk-white walls of Troy.
ELECTRA   And so it was!
AEGISTHUS   You will not learn, my poor Electra.
   Your father and his brother did not have the nerve to stay
   And die like kings, nor yet to go and seek their fortunes overseas.
   Their time was up; they ran, but only to the fringes of this realm
   Taking Iphigenia as hostage and sought to bargain for her life
   Against a plot of land to settle on in Aulis.

ELECTRA   That is not true. The winds would not permit their passage.
AEGISTHUS   The oracles, the omens, now the winds!
   I suppose their oarsman had the palsy.
   But what a favourable omen for departure,
   What a welcome wind arose,
   When up stormed Clytaemnestra with her fighting men.
   You should know your mother's anger
   When the laws are not observed – especially those which govern conduct in the Royal House itself.
   Away they went to Troy, for better the deep sea
   Than the anger of a Queen.
   His time was up and Agamemnon ran!
   And that, dear child, is why you never will be Queen.
ELECTRA   And your time – is that not nearly done?
   You will have cause enough to run when once you hear my news.
AEGISTHUS   I will not run.
ELECTRA   Brave words! A man with little nerve may well consent
   To drink the poppy-loaded wine and stagger, uncomprehending to the axe
   But can that man in full possession of his wits, pick up a sword
   And battle for his life?
AEGISTHUS   A pointless question, child. I go consenting.
   They will not have to drag me to finality.
ELECTRA   You fool, you do not understand.
   Troy is down!
AEGISTHUS   Troy, Athens, Thebes or Babylon – what are they to me?
ELECTRA   Troy is down! Troy is down! And Agamemnon now returns.
   My father is coming home!
   Run, run Aegisthus, let him not find you in my mother's bed!
AEGISTHUS   His life is forfeit in Mycenae by our laws. How can he come?

ELECTRA   If he has men enough to follow him, and they have
      power enough to ransack Troy,
   He can make new laws to his choosing here.
AEGISTHUS   And so, in time, Electra would be Queen.
   Or would she? What of your sisters?
ELECTRA   Why does your mind not comprehend the sounds
      your ears collect?
   We talk of kings, not queens.
AEGISTHUS   But Agamemnon has no male child to his name
   Unless he's fathered bastards on the maids of Troy.
   How will you know these demi-brethren of yours?
   By the colour of their hair?
ELECTRA   Any man who puts a sword into your side will I call
      brother.
   But why should I need to look outside my blood for help
   Even to those with only half my blood.
   My father and my mother are not sorry mules
   And yet may bring a king into this world.
AEGISTHUS   Your mother willing!
ELECTRA   Why not? She will see things differently when
      Father comes again.
AEGISTHUS   Then I shall meet him sword in hand!
   Why do you think I choose the axe except to make my
      daughter Queen?
   There will be no new laws in this land.
ELECTRA   Run, Aegisthus, run!
AEGISTHUS   Steward!
(*Enter* STEWARD)
STEWARD (*to* ELECTRA)   You should not be here!
AEGISTHUS   Throw this woman out and then return to me.
 STEWARD   Come now! Not in the throne room, surely you
      must know.
(STEWARD *bustles* ELECTRA *out.*)
ELECTRA (*on way out*)   Run, Aegisthus, run!
(*Exit* ELECTRA *and* STEWARD)
AEGISTHUS   She has more spirit than her father had.
   Yet he might now have the courage to attack this realm
   With a loot-fed army at his back.

No, ridiculous! The people would not stand aside to see
Traditions of the centuries thrown down.
Or could he claim a further term of office as the consort of
   the Queen?
A pretty constitutional point.
What of Elena? She would still be Queen-to-be
But only if I die. That's the key – only if I die.
But if I run! Ha! (*mimics* ELECTRA) 'Run, Aegisthus, run,
For here comes Agamemnon, King of Kings,
The man who pulled down Troy, and now would sire the
   future Queen.'
A neat contrivance. Steward!
   (STEWARD *enters*)   Steward, I wanted you.
STEWARD   Ah, yes, so you did. More wine, no doubt.
AEGISTHUS   The Furies take you, man. Listen to me.
   You know my time is nearly up.
STEWARD   Oh yes indeed. Of course I'll have your baggage
      packed.
   There is a mule-cart you may have.
AEGISTHUS   I'll have you in the shafts of it, you fool.
STEWARD   You may not talk to me like that, Aegisthus,
   For I am Steward to the Queen.
   Pack your own baggage, then, and go on foot.
AEGISTHUS (*slowly and distinctly*)   I do not pack; I do not run
      away.
   I die consenting as the King.
STEWARD (*confused; trying to remember the appropriate
      courtesies*)   Sire, my apologies. I did not know. It's been
      so long.
   What would you have me do?
AEGISTHUS   The couriers and the watch towers round the
      coast:
   Whose responsibility?
STEWARD   Mine, my Lord.
AEGISTHUS   Keep watch for black ships from the east;
   Old, weather-worn, sea-beaten ships that seem to know
   The pattern of the waves and currents off our shores
   Yet show no mark of origin, neither the snake of Attica,

The sting-ray of the Cyclades, the golden eye by which the
   men of Byblos see their way.
The chain of messengers around the coast:
Double it. Keep clear the roads;
Set up beacon flares so Night may never drop her veil
Between the news and me. Mark that! The news comes first
   to me!
Your duty may require you to pass all news to other ears,
But on this one occasion, first to me!
You understand? Good! (*Dismisses* STEWARD).

To Mother Labrys, greetings. Waken from your sleep, old
   crone
And bare your single tooth for here comes sustenance.
   (*Tears down curtain*.)
(*Awed*) Madam, I am – at least I was a little time ago –
A hobbled stallion, a chained bull of Mycenae.
The next-to-nothing consort of the Queen
Who yet would see his daughter on the throne
Though she would make a mockery of other men.
If this must be the law and if there must be Queens
Let them be of my blood, let me long be known as Father of
   Queens
Like old Tyndareus.
You have not slaked your thirst since Perieres died
And he, poor fool, had not a daughter to his name – he is
   forgotten.
But let me be remembered as father of Elena, Queen-to-be.
Nine years I had and they are gone. Wake, Mother Labrys,
Wake from your dust-dry slumbering,
Bite on my neck and make her Queen.
(*Enter* CLYTAEMNESTRA *to* AEGISTHUS, *who rises and
   bows*.)
AEGISTHUS   My Lady.
CLYTAEMNESTRA (*sits on throne*)   Seat yourself, husband.
   (*A pause*.)
Some things are fit for jest and others not,
But this the steward tells me must be true.

(AEGISTHUS *nods assent.*)
    Men are queer creatures, unpredictable; I should have said
    That you had still a taste for life
    And would adapt yourself to change of place and status.
    Yet I am mistaken; you wish your death.
AEGISTHUS   I do not wish my death, my Lady.
    I will go proud and angry to the axe, but I will go
    Because, nine years ago ...
    Because, nine years ago, I wed a woman whom l thought
    Was worth the dying for.
    Time in his crusty way has shown me wrong;
    I have not touched your heart, and even when I warm your bed
    You do not take me as a man, but just according to the precedents.
    If Mycenae's hold on me had just been you
    I would have left a good few years ago.
    But now I have three children,
    One of whom, Elena, could be Queen
    Or could be nothing, like Electra and the rest.
    I have the power – the only power I have – that no-one else possesses
    Not even you; to make her Queen-to-be.
    I choose the axe.
CLYTAEMNESTRA   The exercise of power, how like a man!
    Power is a heady drink to men, that far outstrips the potency of wine
    So much that they would cut out their own throats for the taste of it.
    What do we see in countries ruled by kings? Power and blood, power and blood!
    That is why in all sane countries power is with the Queen.
AEGISTHUS   Your power, my blood.
CLYTAEMNESTRA   How dare you! In your case, a sacrament, freely given,
    Refreshing, renewing, replenishing.
    And you would compare the act of reverence
    With the blood-lusts of the mountain kings where the cry is

'Blood, blood, blood' for the sake of blood.
The one before you wished to be a king – what is he now?
A cut-throat, pirate, outlaw.
He would have been the same had he been King,
Waging war on Thebes or Attica!

AEGISTHUS I am no Agamemnon! True, if you had trusted me
I would have served as Lawgates as faithfully as Perilaus
And only used the army in defence. But, as you did not,
I am content with the one power I have,
To make Elena Queen.
Why rail at me because I choose to act within the precedents?

CLYTAEMNESTRA I have the same desire, to see Elena Queen-to-be.
And I had planned a course of action to that end
Assuming you would leave.
First, my assumptions undermined; then my plan made pointless.
Lastly, my desire achieved by you.
Why should a Queen not storm in circumstances such as these?

AEGISTHUS Without her power, Goddess-on-Earth is but an angry wench!

CLYTAEMNESTRA You must not laugh at me!

AEGISTHUS To punish me, advance the time of sacrifice!

CLYTAEMNESTRA Oh!
All right! You act within the precedents
Though it is one which I would rather see fall into desuetude
And be abandoned.

AEGISTHUS Thank you, my Lady.

CLYTAEMNESTRA Hmm.

AEGISTHUS There is something else?

CLYTAEMNESTRA Hmm. What did you say a while ago?
What was your reason?

AEGISTHUS For what, madam?

CLYTAEMNESTRA You said, nine years ago, the reason why you chose
To take your place beside me on the throne . . .

AEGISTHUS   The love of ceremonial; delight in royal
      formalities.
CLYTAEMNESTRA   I think too much ceremonial and formality
   Has closed my eyes to worthwhile truths.
   What else could I do? I am the Queen.
AEGISTHUS   If I had my time again, my Lady ...
CLYTAEMNESTRA   It would be the same.
AEGISTHUS   No, for now I know you can be hoisted on your
      precedents;
   Then you leave your point of isolation – remote, aloof, and
      queenly –
   Becoming human in your anger, becoming woman,
   One who could be goaded to the edge of tears, then nursed,
      then comforted, then ...
CLYTAEMNESTRA   Yes?
AEGISTHUS   If I had my time again.
CLYTAEMNESTRA   Do not treat me thus. I am the Queen.
AEGISTHUS   You are angry again! I have found the key!
CLYTAEMNESTRA   Yes, Aegisthus, you have found the key,
   too late to use it.
AEGISTHUS   You are the Queen again. So be it! Strike true!
CLYTAEMNESTRA   I can do that; you cannot touch my
   feelings at the sacrifice
   For Mother Labrys rules me then.
AEGISTHUS   I know, I will go consenting.
(*Exit* CLYTAEMNESTRA.)
(*Enter* TYNDAREUS *and* PERILAUS.)
TYNDAREUS   My Lord Aegisthus; we have heard ... that is,
   we understand ...
AEGISTHUS   I know what you have heard by the way you now
   address me.
TYNDAREUS   It is true, then? I don't know what to say.
AEGISTHUS   Had you no speech prepared for this eventuality?
TYNDAREUS   It is such a long time since ... (*Sees torn curtain
   and Mother Labrys*)
   No-one may see her yet (*Goes to replace curtain*)
PERILAUS   Wait! So this is the Maker of Queens.
   Never in my life have I seen her openly –

Just a shadow on the curtain, never more, till now.
Never in my life have I seen her at her work ...
AEGISTHUS   I trust I shall complete your education, Perilaus,
To your bloody satisfaction.
(PERILAUS *releases hold on* TYNDAREUS *who replaces the curtain as best he can.*)
PERILAUS   No offence intended, Lord Aegisthus. It will be a noble end.
Well, we must get busy, there is a lot to do.
The ceremony is intricate ...
AEGISTHUS   Would you have me rehearse my part?
PERILAUS   Not while there are slaves and felons to act as substitute!
TYNDAREUS   Come, gentlemen, this is no place for bickering.
My Lord Aegisthus, you have a choice to make.
AEGISTHUS   I have chosen. I stay.
TYNDAREUS   No not that, a further choice.
(*Indicates curtain*)   This is not the only way,
And for my daughter's sake, I hope you will choose otherwise.
AEGISTHUS   What other way?
TYNDAREUS   A challenger may come, and in single combat, end your days.
AEGISTHUS   And if no-one comes?
TYNDAREUS   Sometimes a stranger has been known to make a bidding for the throne. If not,
We have to see to it that someone to our choice appears.
AEGISTHUS   And if I strike him down?
PERILAUS   Rest assured that will not happen; we see to that.
AEGISTHUS   Ah, a weakened sword, slow poison in my wine.
Indeed, the ceremony is intricate.
Wait, you said a challenger ... any challenger?
Has Electra put this notion in your heads?
TYNDAREUS   Electra?
PERILAUS   What has she to do with this?
TYNDAREUS   This is a custom long established. But why Electra?
PERILAUS   You think little of the Queen's Councillors if you think we pay attention to that slut.

AEGISTHUS   This is my choice, the Lady or the challenger?
    No other way?
PERILAUS   No other way, my Lord.
AEGISTHUS   I choose the axe; as soon as it may be.
    There is no need to seek a challenger.
(AEGISTHUS *exits*.)
TYNDAREUS (*after* AEGISTHUS *leaves*)   There is a point,
    dear Perilaus, I think you've overlooked.
    An academic one, no doubt, but still it is another choice.
    Well, no, 'choice' is not the word – 'possibility' perhaps.
PERILAUS   If there are hairs to split, call in Tyndareus!
TYNDAREUS   Precision, my boy, and accuracy should be our
    attributes as Councillors.
PERILAUS   Trot out your possibility and let me see it take this
    fence.
TYNDAREUS   A willing substitute of equal blood.
PERILAUS   A what! Ho, a sorry beast, indeed!
    Still, I must concede your point; there is a precedent,
    Though even that I find a trifle hard to masticate.
    A moral tale more than a principle of law.
TYNDAREUS   It is a valid precedent.
PERILAUS   Well yes, but there the motive sprang from
    comradeship,
    Brothers in arms, a noble chivalry ...
    Who would give up his life to save this puppet, this
    semblance of a man?
    Name me just one to call Aegisthus 'Friend'.
TYNDAREUS   That is not the point. If we forget or overlook
    the precedent
    Because it does not seem to touch Aegisthus
    Then are we, or our successors, like to overlook it
    When a more worthy consort comes to die.
PERILAUS   You are right, of course.
TYNDAREUS   We are the guardians of all the precedents
    Not just the few which seem applicable.
PERILAUS   Of course, of course.
TYNDAREUS   Otherwise our judgements would be personal,
    As if we were the rulers of this land and makers of its laws

And that would never do.
Eh? Perilaus, I said ...
PERILAUS   Of course, of course.
(*Enter* STEWARD)
STEWARD   Excuse me, Lords ...
TYNDAREUS   Ah yes?
STEWARD   I would like to verify ... that is, if Lord Aegisthus is to ...
I mean, is he now entitled to the same ... courtesies ...
TYNDAREUS   As is the Queen. That is so.
PERILAUS   He is smartly off the mark, is King Aegisthus! Wants to make the most of it, his trifling span of time!
STEWARD   Yes, indeed. Already has he ordered me ...
PERILAUS   Ordered!
TYNDAREUS   Here's the one who knows his precedents!
PERILAUS   And what does the King, our master, want? More wine?
STEWARD   It makes no sense!
PERILAUS   To you, no doubt. Perhaps to us ...
STEWARD   'Watch for black ships from the east ...
Hasten the news ... but first to me.'
TYNDAREUS   That has the quality of an oracle.
Black ships ... east ... this needs interpreting;
Crows against a rising sun. Hmm. Presentiments of death.
Excuse me, Perilaus, I must do some research on this problem.
Unless you have the meaning, eh? Oh well. (*Exit* TYNDAREUS)
PERILAUS   To me it means 'black ships from the east.'
Aegisthus, whatever else he does, spends little time on dreams.
Steward! What news came to Lord Aegisthus recently?
STEWARD   None, sir. The messengers report to me.
PERILAUS   Always? Some news has reached him first ...
STEWARD   Ah, Electra!
PERILAUS   Electra?
STEWARD   I found the wanton in the Throne Room: I saw her off!
PERILAUS   What had she to say to Lord Aegisthus?

STEWARD   She kept on screaming 'Run, Aegisthus, run'
   And laughing. Mad!
PERILAUS   Hm, not so mad, but well-informed, maybe.
   It seems we are not the only persons in this land
   To run a chain of messengers.
   And the news that reached Electra?
   Tell me, Steward, what is the news from our eastern ports?
STEWARD   Nothing of importance, sir.
   A foundering ship; a better price for skins
   The Euxine trader overdue; the Syrian on time.
   Oh yes, he said he saw a plume of smoke . . .
PERILAUS   Ah! Now let me think . . . against Mount Ida,
      probably?
STEWARD   Oh, you've heard? A forest fire, no doubt.
   And then a monstrous fish on the harbour wall at Paphos . . .
PERILAUS   Yes, yes, I'm sure.
   I did not guess he had the strength . . .
STEWARD   Oh, but it's dead, sir. Thrown up by the waves . . .
PERILAUS   Shush, man! Raiding, yes, and piracy . . .
STEWARD   No news of pirates, sir.
PERILAUS   In the name of the Mother, be silent!
   Now, have you sent word to the eastern ports as Lord
      Aegisthus asked?
   Not yet? See to it now, and then straight back to me.
(*Exit* STEWARD)
   So Agamemnon, he who ran away, now has the means to
      throw down Troy
   And loot its deep-sunk treasuries.
   But Troy is not just Troy, but also tributary to the Phrygian
   And Mitas will not stand aside and watch another steal its
      gold.
   When Phrygia is roused not even Agamemnon is secure
      upon that coast,
   Though he had power to sack a dozen Troys.
   Suppose he were to say 'I shall be King in Troy
   And rule this land as Priam did' –
   How long would it take for Phrygia to change his mind
   And send him packing? Ten days?

How long the Syrian with his news? How long the fires a-
burning e'er he saw the smoke?
Ten days again, maybe.
And news already to Electra for, if I read the signs aright,
Her message to Aegisthus was 'Run Aegisthus run!
For Agamemnon comes, and would be King again'.
Despite no precedent? What did that boor ever care for
precedent?
He slew the child of Tantalus – why even Tantalus died out
of turn!
I could oppose him on the shore and probably match
strength for strength
But can I match gold for gold? Who's been bought and
who's been sold?
Let us suppose, Perilaus, that you have been undermined,
Ah yes, a weakened sword, slow poison in your wine.
And all your army cries, 'Hail Agamemnon.'
(*Re-enter* STEWARD)
Ah good. Now, when the news of black ships reaches you
Come straight to me.
STEWARD   Excuse me, sir. I am bound by Lord Aegisthus to
take the news
Direct to him.
PERILAUS (*aside*)   H'm. A gold-diverted tongue, maybe.
  (*to* STEWARD)   Of course, that is required of you. But
after that, come straight to me.
STEWARD   It shall be so.
PERILAUS   See to it also, that, when these black ships enter port
Their captain hears these words:
From Perilaus, Leader of the Men, greetings!
A friendship unto death which makes a man a king.
STEWARD   Your pardon, Lord. I did not catch the sense.
PERILAUS   Ignore the sense, but word for word deliver it:
From Perilaus, Leader of the Men, greetings!
A friendship unto death which makes a man a king.
Repeat it so!
STEWARD   From Perilaus, Leader of the Men, greetings!
A friendship unto death which makes a man a king.

(PERILAUS *motions* STEWARD *away as* TYNDAREUS *re-enters.* STEWARD *exits.*)
TYNDAREUS   What was that? ... Makes a man a king?
   I thought they had forgotten that old ceremonial cry!
   The welcome to the willing substitute, eh?
   Fancy the Steward remembering it!
   Still, there's little chance of making use of it ...
   Well, now, these black ships from the east;
   Do you know, I really think he meant just what he said ...
   Have you heard? The Euxine trader's overdue.
   Aegisthus must be looking for some import ...
   Though what, in circumstances such as this, I cannot think.
   A parting gift, perhaps, a prize to be competed for in honour of his death.
PERILAUS   That's it! How to separate one man from ten thousand men.
   A chariot race ...
TYNDAREUS   Ah yes!
PERILAUS (*aside*)   ... with only one team made available.
   (*to* TYNDAREUS)   I will add to the prize; it may be in his life I have not been fair enough to Lord Aegisthus
   So let this be a glorious tribute to his dying.
   Let every chariot in the land come to the games!
TYNDAREUS   You know, at first I thought you were exaggerating,
   Speaking of ten thousand in a race, but now I'm not so sure.
   This will be a spectacle! Will you compete?
PERILAUS   Not for my own prize, surely?
   Anyway, it had crossed my mind – if it does not offend some precedent
   To lend my team to Lord Aegisthus for his final ride.
   After all, it is the chariot from which the Leader of the Men commands the army of Mycenae
   And on that one day in his life, I acknowledge his supremacy.
TYNDAREUS   Nobly said, my friend. It shall be so.
PERILAUS   So for the races afterwards
   I think it would be tactful if my chariot was – not available.

TYNDAREUS   True, true. Then you will join me for the judging?
PERILAUS   If all goes well.
   You will promulgate the rules and set the course?
TYNDAREUS   Ten thousand chariots! Oh dear, this will take some organising.
PERILAUS   Or would you rather ...
TYNDAREUS   Yes, you do it, Perilaus. I have not raced a chariot for years.
   And you should have more recent knowledge of the game.
PERILAUS   Thank you, Lord Tyndareus. The scene is set.

HISTORICAL NOTE

As the chariot carrying Agamemnon approached the palace, a royal carpet was unrolled and Clytaemnestra, in her majesty, came forward to give a royal greeting.

She led him to the royal bath house beside the palace where a warm and perfumed bath had been prepared for him. After he had bathed, he put one foot out of the silver bath and as he did so, Clytaemnestra came forward proffering a golden apple. As he bit upon it, she threw over him a silver net. He was then slain with the sacrificial axe.

Thus he died, neither on land nor on water, neither in his palace nor outside it, neither clothed nor unclothed, neither fasting nor eating, neither rich nor poor.

The king is dead, long live the king.

The precedents have been observed.

THE UNIFICATION

CHARACTERS

Watchman
Trophonius
Thalamatas
Orestes
Pylades
Marshall
Electra
Hermione
Steward
Kerewos (*Lawgates*)
Councillor
Telandros
Captain of the Guard (*Lawgates*)

Of Mycenae

Elena
Erigone
Perilaus
Nicostratus
Aletes (*Lawgates*)

Gang of Kids
Crowd of People
Maids

ACT 1

SCENE: *An entrance framed by enormous walls. A* WATCHMAN *looks up at the walls.* TROPHONIUS *is standing by.*

WATCHMAN   'Oo built them walls? Them girt stone walls. 'Oo lifted un
  An' stood un end on end. An' fitted like me fingers fit me 'and.
  Why, I couldn' get a spear point in between them blocks.
  Me father said his father's dad – the one that was at Troy –
  Had helped to build the sentry-walk that marches on the walls –
  But not the walls. 'Oo built them walls?

TROPHONIUS   It's no use asking me. I wasn't there.
  Ah! Here comes the first business of the day. Guess who?
(*Enter* THALAMATAS, *an old limping man.*)
THALAMATAS   Greetings, friends!
WATCHMAN   'Ow do?
TROPHONIUS   'Ow do? From the Guardian of the Gate, 'ow do?
  Have you no sense of purpose or of destiny? (*falsetto*)
  Halt, I say, halt, in the Queen's name! Halt!
  Declare your name and rank and business in this town.
WATCHMAN   Disappear!
THALAMATAS   I should have thought all these particulars were well enough known
  From the dogs that sniff the rubbish dumps up to the Queen herself.
TROPHONIUS   Do not scorn the dogs of Argos; there is more treasure to be found
  By sniffing dumps than moaning drear petitions to the Queen.

37

THALAMATAS   I want justice!
WATCHMAN   Steady now.
TROPHONIUS   You want a new head!
THALAMATAS   For twenty years I've lived by begging charity around the farm I bought!
   They are my fields, my flocks, yet I am driven off with sticks.
   My grandsons stone me and cry 'You're dead! You're dead!'
TROPHONIUS   And so you are, according to the law.
WATCHMAN   It be right foolish, though. Just look at un.
THALAMATAS   That's what I say! That's what I tell the Queen!
   Look at me, Madam! Am I not alive? Did I not serve your father?
(*Distant trumpets.* WATCHMAN *gets up.*)
TROPHONIUS   That's a silly thing to say.
THALAMATAS   It touches her. I know it does. But always the Keeper of the Precedents
   Proclaims me dead once more.
   Look at me! Do I not live?
TROPHONIUS   I would reserve judgement on that point.
(WATCHMAN *opens the gates.*)
   What have you done in twenty years to make a new life for yourself,
   To cloak the past and bite your tongue
   Before it boasts the indiscretions of your youth?
THALAMATAS   I was a soldier!
(CHILD *comes out, sees* THALAMATAS *and runs back.*)
TROPHONIUS   You were an outlaw!
WATCHMAN   Can't you two be silent for a while.
   Hey! Strangers!
(*Enter* ORESTES *with* PYLADES *cautiously They stop at a distance, watching.*)
   Halt! I say, halt! In the Queen's ...
(*He becomes aware that* Trophonius *is miming beside him.*)
   Disappear, can't you? I have a job to do.
(*Enter a gang of kids.*)

KID 1 (*striking attitude before* THALAMATAS)   There were
   the brazen gates
   There were the milk-white walls of Troy.
REST OF THE KIDS (*chanting*)   Take your dirty hands off our
   walls.
KID 1   I have thee, Troy!
REST OF THE KIDS (*chanting*)   Take your dirty hands ...
(THALAMATAS *sweeps about him with his stick and all except*
   KID 1 *run back through the gates.* KID 1 *backs up
   towards* ORESTES.)
KID 1 (*with an exaggerated limp*)   I cannot run or jump as once
   I did – ow!
(ORESTES *gets* KID 1 *by the ear.*)
ORESTES   Kin of yours?
THALAMATAS (*advances on* KID 1, *then halts*)   Let it go! I've
   never hit a prisoner yet.
(KID 1 *backs away from* ORESTES.)
KID 1   You smelly mountain goat! Maa! Maa!
(KID 1 *backs into* PYLADES.)
ORESTES   Careful, friend.
(PYLADES *strikes* KID 1 *viciously, sends* KID 1 *off right.*)
WATCHMAN   Hey! There b'aint no need for stuff as that!
ORESTES   Excuse my friend. Accept our apologies, if you can.
THALAMATAS   It was unnecessary, but let it pass.
TROPHONIUS   Welcome to Argos, my bonny mountaineers.
   What have you brought from your snow-capped peaks
   For us to feast our eyes upon?
   Gold, garnet, topaz, silver; I give a fair price.
   These men will vouch for me – I am a fair dealer.
ORESTES   Wait, man. You talk too quickly.
   Think you I can comprehend your words?
TROPHONIUS (*slower*)   You have stuff to sell? (*opens wallet*)
   See, gold? Silver? To sell?
ORESTES   I am no market bargainer! And do not hiss at me.
WATCHMAN   Ho! The frog and the snake had an argument ...
WATCHMAN & TROPHONIUS   Brek-kek-kek ssss gulp!
   (*laugh*)
ORESTES   You mock me?

THALAMATAS   It is an old fable, a sight too bitter in my view,
   That the Snake Mother gobbles up you Northerners
   With your clacking dialect.
ORESTES   Witch-craft! No snake will feed on me. (*Hand on sword*)
WATCHMAN   Steady, now.
   Oh yes! Declare your name and ... (*sees* TROPHONIUS *miming him again*)
   ... and ... and parentage ... and ...
   What d'ye want in Argos?
TROPHONIUS   You'll never earn promotion, going on like that.
ORESTES   We seek work.
TROPHONIUS   Butchers, by the look of you. (*falsetto*)
   Your name and parentage.
WATCHMAN   Stand aside! This is my job.
   Well, you two. Name and ... parentage.
PYLADES   Keep quiet. It is a trick.
ORESTES   To catch my line of life? And cut or capture it? (*to* WATCHMAN)
   I will have no witchcraft.
WATCHMAN   Please yourselves. You must satisfy the Marshall when he comes.
TROPHONIUS   You're searching for a job, you say?
   Why not enlist as seamen in the fishing fleet. (*laughs*)
ORESTES   On a boat? No, thank you, not my kind of work.
TROPHONIUS (*laughs*)   No, I fancy not.
   Never yet did a mountain-climber love the sea.
ORESTES   I do not like these Argive jibes. (*hand on sword again*)
THALAMATAS   Peace, friend. One learns to live with jests against the Northern blood.
ORESTES   Do you speak from experience?
THALAMATAS   My father was a Northerner, so I am half and half.
   Snake Mother has her fangs in me but neither will she let me be assimilated, nor will she let me go.
   I am neither live nor dead.

PYLADES   I do not like this talk.
THALAMATAS   No, it is not sorcery, but just according to the
     precedents.
ORESTES   Why were those urchins making mock of you?
THALAMATAS   I was at Troy.
ORESTES   Troy? What's Troy?
THALAMATAS   Is she so soon forgotten?
     Are her fallen walls so overgrown with nettles,
     Her ravaged palaces so buried in the dust
     That men can scratch their heads and query 'Troy?'
     Was our victory so parochial that word has not reached back
        unto the limits of this world?
     Why, men of your blood must have been within our
        gathering!
     Were not your fathers or your grandsires in our throng?
PYLADES   Watch it! He wants to know our parentage.
THALAMATAS   Oh, what's the use. It is a dream that old men
     dream.
ORESTES   Wait. There was this stronghold which you
     conquered?
     Why do they mock a man for that?
THALAMATAS   I thought the children might take pride in
     valiant deeds
     And told them many tales. But now I am discredited
     And people laugh at me.
ORESTES   A well-told tale of battle still gets a hearing up in ...
     Where we come from. A fighter still is honoured in his age.
     The King would see to that.
THALAMATAS   This is a country ruled by women, where
     kings are told
     Once they have served their term 'Get out! You are
        forbidden in this land'.
     And they and those that follow them are ... nothing.
ORESTES   What is this? Served their term? You mean, when
     they die?
TROPHONIUS   Snake Mother eats their flesh and stews their
     bones.
PYLADES   Come home! This is no land for folks like us.

THALAMATAS   Do not heed him. An idle babbler, a parasite.
TROPHONIUS   But of a family well thought of in this town.
   My father did not chase the thistledown but stayed and
      served the Queen.
THALAMATAS   Thistledown! I brought a fortune home!
   Silver, gold, iron!
   I bought a tidy farm. I bought my son a vineyard on the hill.
   My daughter had the finest brood mares in the land,
   The best that any man could buy.
   And when my foreign wealth was all converted into things
      which clearly had the stamp of Argos on their origin, they
      broke the news to me.
TROPHONIUS   You're dead.
THALAMATAS   Dead.
ORESTES (*to* PYLADES *who is retreating*)   Come back, you
      clod.
   We are hill-folk, unaccustomed to your mockery
   But one thing surely is the truth; a man dies once and only
      once.
   My sword will make a touch-stone for your trickery.
(TROPHONIUS *and* WATCHMAN *jump between.*)
TROPHONIUS   Steady, stranger. You do not understand our
      laws.
   Because our friend here chose to leave this land
   Without permission of the Queen, he is an outlaw.
   Should he return, he is not recognised.
   He has no legal status. To all intents and purposes, he's dead.
(*Trumpet a bit closer.* WATCHMAN *stands at his post. Other
      people join queue behind* ORESTES *and* PYLADES.)
ORESTES   It is a queer land,
   Where legal fiction clamps on common sense.
TROPHONIUS   If you wish to earn your fortunes here in Argos
   Why not serve a stint with me. I'll pay you well.
   First, I will arrange a permit for your residence within the
      city walls
   Then sign you on as labourers.
   You'll need advice on all the laws and precedents. I'll put
      you wise.

(*Enter* MARSHALL *of the Gate*; WATCHMAN *salutes*.)
WATCHMAN   I guard the Northern gate!
MARSHALL   Guardian of the Gate, take ease!
   Well, now. (*sees* THALAMATAS) Well, now, who have we here?
   Still dead, I see! (*laughs immoderately*) Pass, corpse!
(THALAMATAS *starts to go through gate*.)
ORESTES (*to* PYLADES)   I do not like this cockalorum.
(THALAMATAS *pauses to listen*.)
MARSHALL   Eh? Well, now! Two mountain frogs.
   Two stinking hairy mountain frogs. And one that bears a sword.
   Guardian, who are these men?
WATCHMAN   They would not give their names.
MARSHALL   Oh! Stand there! (*calls up next person in the queue while 'covering'* ORESTES *and* PYLADES)
   You! Name and business? Petition? Pass!
   You next! Eh? Pass!
(*Hubbub growing inside city*)
   And you ...
(EX-CONSORT *runs through gate, whipped by* ELECTRA. *Crowd join in reviling him*.)
   Back there! Clear the way!
ELECTRA   Run! Your time is up! Run, you baby!
   Call yourself a prince! Get out of Argos! Run!
   (*drives him off right*)
(*The* CROWD *and the* MARSHALL *rush to look*. THALAMATAS *has come in again and* ORESTES, PYLADES *and* THALAMATAS *form a group, watching, right*.)
THALAMATAS   Thus they chased my master from the town,
   And Argos has another outlaw now.
ORESTES   Was he the king?
THALAMATAS   Well, consort is the proper word. He has served his time.
PYLADES   Was that the Queen, the Mother Snake?
THALAMATAS   The Queen preserves her dignity.
   But that – you will not believe this but it is true –
   That was a Princess of the Royal Blood.

43

ORESTES   Why is she not locked up when her madness takes
   its clutch on her?
THALAMATAS   Madness? She is not ... You have a lot to
   learn of Argos.
(ELECTRA *returns, flicks her whip at* CROWD, *who fall back*.)
ELECTRA   Out of my way!
   (*lashes* ORESTES *who turns, grabs her wrist, twists whip
   from her hand, bends her over his knee and raises his
   hand to spank her.* MARSHALL *rushes up, draws and
   gets sword point to* ORESTES'*s throat*.)
MARSHALL   Hold! Hold! Hold! You Northerner.
   Release her or I thrust.
ORESTES (*quietly*)   Pylades, open wide. (*releases* ELECTRA)
MARSHALL   How dare you lay your hands on one of Royal
   blood.
   Your pardon, Princess, for this incident.
   Guardian! Escort this man ...
ELECTRA   Wait!
(*She raises hand and slaps* ORESTES *lightly on cheek;*
ORESTES *raises his hand and is jumped on again by*
GUARDIAN *and* MARSHALL)
ELECTRA   Let him go! Marshall, let him go! (*they do*)
   I thought your first assault may well have been
   An unconsidered, automatic act,
   But no! You know precisely who I am and what you aimed
   to do.
ORESTES   What kind of country have I come upon
   Where women raise their hands to men?
ELECTRA   Your dialect and creed proclaim your origin behind
   the Corinth Wall
   Welcome, mountaineer! My father came, as you have
   come,
   From the distant mountains
   Seeking a kingdom of his own.
ORESTES   Welcome? With cuts from a whip?
MARSHALL   Answer the Princess with respect!
ELECTRA   Peace, Marshall. This is my business.
   (*to* ORESTES)   Forgive me, friend.

I am accustomed to the milk-and-water men of Apia
Who clear the way and curtsy as I come.
I had forgotten that there still might be some real men in the world.
Did I hurt?
ORESTES (*laughs*)   No! Not a scrap! The skins I wear upon my back
Have taken harder blows from thicker sticks without complaint.
Well, do the laws of Argos permit me the knowledge of your name?
ELECTRA   You of all people ought to know without the telling,
For in your dialect I was named.
Here they call me Princess Amber, from the colour of my hair.
Look! What would you call me?
ORESTES (*slowly*)   Electra.
ELECTRA   Correct! And yours?
MARSHALL   He has refused to say, Princess. Obstinate!
ELECTRA   Who are you, friend?
ORESTES (*slowly*)   I am a mountaineer...
ELECTRA   In your dialect, an orestes, we have had them here before.
One slew my mother...
MARSHALL   So you see, we do not trust you northerners, slayers of queens.
Why should we? You do not honour the Mother and observe our laws.
(*to* ELECTRA) Princess, with your permission, once again I'll ask him for his name and parentage,
And business in this town. If he refuses, I will see him off.
ELECTRA   No, Marshall! Leave the man to me. (*moves down stage from* CROWD)
Orestes, here! (*motions him forward, but he stands firm*)
Your pardon, friend. Would you please come here?
(ORESTES *comes*)
(*quietly*) Tell me, are you a man to kill a queen?

ORESTES   I did not kill your mother! I have newly come into your land.
Never before ...
ELECTRA   Peace, friend. That was years ago and the man that did was hunted down and slain.
Are you a man to kill a queen, and live to tell of it?
ORESTES   I have come to work in Argos and will obey your laws.
If people treat me right, I'll not kill anyone.
ELECTRA   This is no trap I set before you.
My mother sacrificed my father in the name of precedents ...
ORESTES   She killed the king?
ELECTRA   There are no kings in Apia, only consorts of a Queen,
But yes, she killed my father, not in anger or by accident
But coldly with due ritual, ceremoniously she struck him down.
ORESTES   Why? Why? What had he done?
ELECTRA   He had served his time, the nine years as a consort
As our laws provide; just as that weakling who you saw me whip out of the town had served his turn
As consort to the Queen in Argos.
But unlike that coward, my father wished to serve another term.
My mother sought to keep another in her bed
And so my father died.
ORESTES   I could kill a queen like that.
ELECTRA   Orestes, you are a brother to my revenge.
Will you work for me, and I will speak you past the guard?
ORESTES   I am to kill the Queen in Argos? What is my wage?
ELECTRA   No, no, not Hermione. She is my cousin, and though she does not seem to have the inner strength
To break all these abominable precedents
She is minded to. She needs encouragement.
There! That is your wage. Consort to the Queen Hermione, King in Argos if you will.
There must be a choosing of the future consort soon.
What I can do by talking quietly to the Queen, that I will do.
The rest is for your sword.

ORESTES   A goodly wage but yet ... you have not named my
    task.
ELECTRA   I should be High Queen of Mycenae, not that
    imbecile,
  Who sits upon the rights of Atreus and, from afar
  Has put her fingers on my lips so I may never join in public
    business of this realm.
  I am forbidden entrance to the city of my birth
  The country that my father ruled ...
ORESTES   I am to kill that Queen?
ELECTRA   She is the product of adultery, the leavings of the
    beast
  Who fouled my father's bed. Get rid of her.
ORESTES   I will be paid my wages first; then do the job.
ELECTRA   Done.
(*The* MARSHALL *is passing through the other travellers
except* PYLADES, *who seems to be asleep against the
wall*)
ORESTES   Now speak me and my comrade past the guard;
  I am tired of standing here.
ELECTRA   You will not even tell me ... no, no matter.
  I have already named you as Orestes; it will serve,
  A cadet of the House of Atreus – there, we are kinsfolk.
ORESTES   You mentioned Atreus just now; that is an Achaean
    name.
ELECTRA   You know it? I am his grandchild; the only one I
    think
  In which the blood runs true. We were a proud race; be
    worthy of the name.
ORESTES   Lead on.
ELECTRA (*to* MARSHALL)   I have explained our custom to
    this traveller and he will conform.
  I think that you yourself might well have had less trouble
  Had you but shown more courtesy.
MARSHALL   Princess Amber! Is that fair?
ELECTRA   Do your duty, Marshall.
MARSHALL (*looks at* ORESTES *for a while*)   It is the custom
    of our city ...

ORESTES   I know. I am Orestes of the House of Atreus, Lord
     of Achaea
   Come to meet my kin, such as Electra here.
MARSHALL (*looks long at* ORESTES; *then at* ELECTRA; *then
     at* ORESTES)   Pass, my Lord.
   May your visit be successful.
(ELECTRA *and* ORESTES *pass through the gate*)
   Orestes? She said that was a dialect word. For mountaineer.
   The Queen must hear of this.
(MARSHALL *has his back to* PYLADES, *who stabs him and throws him in the guard room.* PYLADES *goes after* ORESTES *and* ELECTRA.)

ACT 2

SCENE 1

SCENE: *Throne room of Argos.* ORESTES *and* PYLADES *stand dressed in Minoan style.*

PYLADES   What's she like?
ORESTES   Older than I thought, beneath the paint, but I can stand it.
     I am not her first, of course.
PYLADES   You can talk!
     Ah well, a small price to pay for luxury.
ORESTES (*calmly*)   You are a stinking Minyan toad!
PYLADES (*laughs*)   I know! (*laughs*)
     Well, you got the Queen. Me for the Princess, now.
ORESTES   Keep off!
PYLADES   Greedy!
     What do you want to be? A king? Or a cowman?
     Anyway, I took a liking to that wench.
ORESTES   Look, if she were just the second best in Argos
     And we were here for good, I'd not object. You've earned her.
     But she reckons, maybe rightly, maybe not,
     That she has claim not just to a single town and half a dozen villages
     But to all the country south of Corinth.
     So treat her as High Queen 'til we know she's not.
PYLADES   But if she is, I bet I know the new High King.
ORESTES   Correct.
PYLADES   Crafty! And me, I get your leavings here in Argos.
ORESTES   Mycenae rules a dozen towns, each with its petty Queen.
     Take your pick!

PYLADES   You got to kill the mad girl first.
ORESTES   How can I? Electra did not tell me her condition
   When we bargained at the gate.
   The Gods protect such creatures, and avenge their deaths.
   We can ... send her into exile – I don't know.
PYLADES   A long march, that!
   Not only does the army of Mycenae stand between,
   But what of the fighting men of Argos?
   They owe allegiance to all Queens, and none to you.
   You cannot even have the guard called out
   Without permission of the Lawgates.
ORESTES   I can change that, the whole town saw me fight the
   other man contending for the throne
   And saw me win.
   All fighting men respect another fighter.
PYLADES   Try that one on the Lawgates. Here he comes.
(*Enter* STEWARD, KEREWOS *and* COUNCILLOR *ceremoniously, but* ORESTES *and* PYLADES *are in their way,* ORESTES *with back to them.* COUNCILLOR *coughs but* ORESTES *stands firm.*)
STEWARD   Make way for the Councillors of the Queen.
ORESTES (*to* PYLADES)   In a room as large as this a hundred
   men might congregate
   And never tread upon each other's toes.
(*Turns to* KEREWOS *and* COUNCILLOR)
   Greetings. Do you not recognise me?
COUNCILLOR   Will you be so good as to retire from this
   place?
   The business of the day is about to commence.
ORESTES   I know.
KEREWOS   It is not the custom for the consort ...
ORESTES   I know.
KEREWOS   Then leave.
ORESTES   If the Queen so wishes.
(MAIDS *try to enter behind* KEREWOS *and* COUNCILLOR *who look round, dart to their places unceremoniously.* MAIDS *go to throne,* ORESTES *and* PYLADES *stand back a bit.*
HERMIONE, *attended by* ELECTRA, *enters.*)

COUNCILLOR   Hail to the Mother; hail to the ...
ORESTES (*comes forward, takes* HERMIONE's *hands.*)   Why, my love, you look so radiant.
Last night I thought you beautiful enough, but now ...
(*to* ELECTRA) What have you done to her?
(*All the* COURTIERS *are caught half-way through elaborate bows, curtsies, etc.*)
HERMIONE   Orestes, silly boy. As the earth is refreshed by the new season's rains
So is the Queen by her new Consort.
ORESTES   Thank you, my love. (*kisses her to everyone's horror.*)
HERMIONE   You'll mess my hair.
(ORESTES *leads her to throne.*)
COUNCILLOR   Hail to the ...
ORESTES   Is that comfortable? No, how could it be? The stone strikes cold.
Steward, a cushion for the Queen!
(STEWARD *gapes, but goes.*)
COUNCILLOR   Hail ... (*but* KEREWOS *stops him*)
KEREWOS (*to* COUNCILLOR)   Let this farce be acted out, without our forced participation.
(STEWARD *returns with cushion and* ORESTES *fusses over* HERMIONE.)
HERMIONE   Proceed, my Councillors.
KEREWOS   Your pardon, Madam! We were waiting for those not concerned in the business of the day to leave.
ORESTES (*to* MAIDS *in waiting*)   You may go now. I will attend your Mistress.
(*Exit* MAIDS)
HERMIONE   Now, my Councillors, proceed.
(KEREWOS *and* COUNCILLOR *look at each other and shrug.*)
COUNCILLOR (*intoning*)   Madam, according to the precedents, the first day of each new year
The Queen gives audience to those, her subjects, who desire her ear.
Madam, hear their pleas.

HERMIONE   Their words shall reach my ears.
   And the first for my attention?
COUNCILLOR (*more naturally; half a smile*)   Almost a precedent himself;
   I need hardly remind you of the case.
(STEWARD *exits*)
HERMIONE   The limping one? Poor man, is there nothing we can do?
COUNCILLOR   Nothing. That is well established.
(STEWARD *returns with* THALAMATAS *who stands before*
HERMIONE *and then tries awkwardly to kneel, one leg stiff.*)
ORESTES (*coming forward*)   My friend, gently now.
   (*to* HERMIONE) Madam, this man was wounded in the service of your father
   And finds it difficult to kneel. To show he means no disrespect
   Let me kneel for him, while he presents his case.
HERMIONE   Dear Orestes! Yes, let it be so.
THALAMATAS   My Lady, hear my plea.
HERMIONE   Your words fall on my ears.
THALAMATAS   Madam, you know me; I was your father's bodyguard
   And in his service . . .
COUNCILLOR   Yes, yes. You may assume the Queen knows all the facts.
THALAMATAS   . . . restore my land to me. The farm I bought.
HERMIONE (*gently*)   Your case has been decided, many years ago.
COUNCILLOR   In the matter of the White Grape Farm, there being but one claimant to possession . . .
THALAMATAS   What about me? I paid for it.
COUNCILLOR   You left this realm without permission and lost your civil rights.
   You are non-existent, legally.
THALAMATAS   I paid for it. King Menelaus knew that.
COUNCILLOR   Madam, the usual formula, I think.
HERMIONE (*to* THALAMATAS, *gently*)   I'm sorry.
ORESTES   My Lady, hear my plea.

HERMIONE   Your words fall ... You, Orestes? What plea?
ORESTES   Here is a man who served your father well.
   If some legal trickery prevents him having what is his,
   Can you not, in your bounty, grant him a living
   Somewhere in the Royal House, as guard or watchman,
   If only as a token of your father's memory.
HERMIONE   Dear Orestes!
COUNCILLOR   Madam.
HERMIONE   Yes, my Councillor?
COUNCILLOR   A man who has no civil rights can hardly seal a
   contract with your Steward here.
   Non-suited, if it please my Lady.
HERMIONE   Oh dear.
ORESTES   My Lady, may I make another plea?
COUNCILLOR   No. The Queen has not pronounced upon your
   first.
ORESTES   My Lady, may I employ a serving man?
HERMIONE   Oh yes. Of course. At least ... (to
   COUNCILLOR) Can he?
COUNCILLOR   No valid contract can be made.
ORESTES   That is my burden.
KEREWOS   What does he want with a serving man?
   Are there not enough servants in the Palace for the Consort?
ORESTES   That is my burden.
HERMIONE   Well, can he?
COUNCILLOR   My Lady, legally ... (*shrugs*)
HERMIONE   Lord Orestes, your words fall on my ears ... and
   please me.
ORESTES   Thank you, my love.
   (*to* THALAMATAS) Stand by me, friend.
COUNCILLOR (*coughs*)   Madam, I think that man should
   leave ...
ORESTES   What man?
COUNCILLOR   That man! Thalamatas.
ORESTES   Legally, I see no man.
HERMIONE (*laughs*)   Councillor, do I see any man – legally?
KEREWOS (*to* COUNCILLOR)   It seems we underestimate the
   opposition.

COUNCILLOR   We should not ask petitioners to state their case before this mob.
KEREWOS   What else is in the list? Ah ...
That should be interesting.
HERMIONE   My Councillors. What is next for my attention?
COUNCILLOR (*to* STEWARD)   Advance this case.
(*Exit* STEWARD)
(*to* HERMIONE) My Lady; in the matter of the slaying of the Marshall of the Northern Gate.
The accused, by the name Trophonius, failing to answer satisfactorily
Now comes before you for his sentence.
(*Enter* STEWARD, TROPHONIUS *and* GUARDS)
My Lady, as to the slaying of the Marshall, hear the evidence.
One: the accused was seen leaving the place where the Marshall was slain
Simultaneously with the finding of the corpse.
HERMIONE (*to* TROPHONIUS)   Is the evidence agreed?
TROPHONIUS   My Lady, yes but I was but passing. I saw no corpse.
HERMIONE (to COUNCILLOR)   Proceed.
COUNCILLOR   Two: on his arrest, the accused was in possession of certain precious goods
Gold, silver and the like, such as should have been declared on entry.
That he is not licensed as a dealer in such goods;
That the goods were not declared.
HERMIONE (*to* TROPHONIUS)   Is the evidence agreed?
TROPHONIUS   My Lady, yes, I had these goods – but is that proof of murder?
HERMIONE (*to* COUNCILLOR)   Proceed.
COUNCILLOR   The inference, my Lady, is that being challenged by the Marshall,
The accused, rather than suffer confiscation of his goods, did slay the Marshall.
HERMIONE (*to* TROPHONIUS)   And your defence?
TROPHONIUS   I did not see the Marshall. I was not stopped. I never am.

They know me at the Gate. I was only passing through, my
   Lady.
HERMIONE   Hear my decision...
ORESTES   My love, one moment.
   (*to* COUNCILLOR) No other fact?
(COUNCILLOR *looks stonily ahead*)
   No weapon?
(COUNCILLOR *will not answer to* ORESTES)
HERMIONE (*to* COUNCILLOR)   No weapon?
COUNCILLOR   My Lady, a search was made, but
   unsuccessfully.
HERMIONE   What.... sort of implement was used?
COUNCILLOR (*to* KEREWOS)   This is your province.
KEREWOS   A short blade, my Lady, but unusual: tapering,
   ribbed.
ORESTES (*to* KEREWOS, *drawing but merely showing*)   Like
   that?
(KEREWOS *draws smartly, knocks dagger from* ORESTES'*s
hand, and puts his point at* ORESTES'*s throat*)
KEREWOS   How dare you draw a weapon in the presence of
   the Queen?
ORESTES   Pylades, open wide!
(PYLADES *makes no move*)
KEREWOS   Your foreign gods cannot assist you now for here
   the Mother reigns.
HERMIONE (*to* KEREWOS)   Stop it at once. I do not need
   protection from Orestes.
   This is excess of zeal!
KEREWOS   Your pardon, my Lady.
(*Puts away sword; picks up* ORESTES's *dagger*)
   Ah yes. A Parnassian blade; I know it now.
   (*to* HERMIONE) My Lady, with such a weapon was the
   Marshall slain.
HERMIONE   Are you implying... Orestes...
ELECTRA   This is madness. I was with Orestes...
COUNCILLOR   Princess! Please, this is public business!
ORESTES   It would seem the Princess wants to speak for me
   Yet you would prevent her testimony.

What sort of justice do you dispense, old man,
    What sort of trial that hears the prosecutor, but not the words of witnesses?
COUNCILLOR   My Lord, it is this man here on trial, not you!
ORESTES   The Lawgates claims it was my weapon that struck your Marshall down,
    But now you will not hear Electra speak for me.
COUNCILLOR   Please, please. I make no allegation pointing to your guilt in this.
    Princess Amber may not speak for other reasons that antedate your coming to this realm.
ORESTES   A cunning trick, these unknown reasons, to leave my name besmirched.
COUNCILLOR   My Lord Orestes! This is by order of Mycenae!
    The High Queen, she who sent the Princess here,
    Laid down that from all public business must her ladyship abstain,
    And never join her voice in argument.
ORESTES   And so I am condemned!
HERMIONE   We cannot leave the matter just like this!
    I must hear what Amber has to say. I must!
COUNCILLOR   My Lady, the High Queen has forbidden it.
HERMIONE   I will hear it not as public business but privately.
    It shall not be written down.
    Amber, you were saying?
ELECTRA   I was with Orestes
    From the time the Marshall passed us at the Gate until we reached the Palace here,
    This I swear, upon the Mother. He never left my side. And this man lies!
KEREWOS   Princess Amber, please! I merely said 'with such a weapon...'
    I did not specify...
ORESTES (*to* HERMIONE)   My Lady, may I speak?
HERMIONE   Proceed, Orestes dear! He has not hurt you, has he now?
ORESTES   Surprised, not hurt.

There is another point. This learned gentleman has said
That gold and silver, and kindred riches were found upon
   this man
Who had no right to carry them. Correct?
(COUNCILLOR *does not reply*)
HERMIONE (*to* COUNCILLOR)   Answer, please.
COUNCILLOR   That is so.
ORESTES   Tell me please! Was there a golden bangle, worked
   with snakes?
   Two golden ear-rings, each with three eagles hanging from a
      chain,
   A silver ring, entwined the way girls plait their hair.
   All in a leather wallet, so big, tooled with an interlaced design
   Oh yes, carnelians unmounted, and other stones . . .
COUNCILLOR   Well now, yes, I think . . .
   (*to* STEWARD) Would you mind?
(STEWARD *exits quickly*)
ORESTES (*to* HERMIONE)   You did not think, my love, that I
   would come to pay you court
   Without a bride-gift in my hand.
   Oh yes, you must have thought
   How lowly has the House of Atreus become that it must
      send its princes out like paupers,
   Like begging men.
HERMIONE   Oh no!
ORESTES   Who would blame you? When Electra led me to
   your side
   I had nothing.
   You would have thought me such a fool if I had said
   'I have lost the gifts I bring.'
(*Re-enter* STEWARD *with wallet*)
   That's it! And here! A golden bangle worked with snakes!
   It looks much better on your arm.
   These ear-rings! Can you feel the eagles swooping on your
      cheeks?
   This silver ring. Wear it for me, my love.
(*Goes to* TROPHONIUS)
   My friend! My honest friend! You found my little treasury

    And hurried after me?
    You have pleased me. Better, you have pleased the Queen.
TROPHONIUS   Oh, yes!
ORESTES (*to* COUNCILLOR)   And now, my learned friend,
    what of your inference?
    Do you now say that such a man, burdened with so much
        honesty
    Would murder anyone who stood between him and his wish
        to restore another's property?
    Is there not a better case against Orestes?
    His gold, his silver, undeclared, not licensed as a dealer,
    His sword?
HERMIONE   Peace, my sweet. We know that is not true.
    And you, the accused, I would free you from the charge.
    Is it agreed, my Councillors?
KEREWOS   }
COUNCILLOR   } Agreed: agreed.
ORESTES   My Queen, I would have this honest man to join my
        little company of friends.
    I would entrust what little fortune I have left,
    These uncut stones, to his safe custody.
HERMIONE   Of course, my love.
ORESTES   Stand there; you are in good company.
HERMIONE   And the next for my attention?
ORESTES   You look magnificent, my dear.
    Enough of legal argument! Let me show you to your people
    That they may see what a lucky man I am.
    (*to* TROPHONIUS) Friend! Find me a chariot! The Queen
        rides out!
HERMIONE (*to* ORESTES)   Oh yes! (*to* COUNCILLOR) We
    have finished?
COUNCILLOR   Well ... (*looks at tablet*)
HERMIONE   Good! Let my words be written down.
COUNCILLOR   They will be set among the precedents.
    But Madam ...
ORESTES   Come, my love! And you Electra, ride with us!
(*All stream out except* KEREWOS *and* PYLADES.
COUNCILLOR *comes last, protesting*)

COUNCILLOR   But Madam . . .
(PYLADES *still sprawls on steps as if asleep*)
KEREWOS (*at salute*)   Argos in disarray! (*sheaths sword*)
    Three things have kept this country whole and sane through countless years;
    The discipline of its arms, the precedents of the law and the majesty of its Queens.
    But the Queen is hung with golden baubles and plays the child
    While the precedents are treated with disdain.
    So from its arms must Argos seek support
    And if this foolishness can not be driven out, having the Queen's blessing as it does
    Then see it is held within its proper place: the confines of her bed.
(*He starts to go; then bends and picks up something; brings it downstage*)
    A little golden eagle, pendant from a chain!
    The consort's presents are as unsubstantial as himself!
(*Starts off again, then checks, and looks more closely*)
    This is not Parnassian workmanship, more like our own.
(PYLADES *draws dagger*)
    Or from the Cretan treasuries. The Palace staff shall trace its origins for me.
(*Starts off again, sees* PYLADES *sprawling on steps*)
    Hey you, arouse yourself! You can't sleep . . . (*sees dagger*) . . . Ah!
(PYLADES *strikes him down*)

ACT 2

SCENE 2

SCENE: *As Scene 1.* THALAMATAS *and three more strangers gossiping.* ORESTES *and* PYLADES *down.*

PYLADES   Bloody disgusting, if you ask me.
ORESTES   It's their fashion; they think nothing of it.
PYLADES   How you feel about yours, well, that's your affair, but me ...
    I'll not have my woman walking around like that.
ORESTES   Take it quietly, Pylades.
    As yet, our feet are not in the chariot straps
    And others hold the reins.
PYLADES   Not so many as there were.
ORESTES   Thanks to you, my friend.
PYLADES   Well, just remember, when you've finished playing kings and queens,
    I want Electra. I could do that girl a power of good.
ORESTES (*coldly*)   You are a vulgar, stinking Minyon toad!
PYLADES (*laughs*)   I like it that way.
(*Enter* TROPHONIUS *and* TELANDROS)
TROPHONIUS   My Lord Orestes!
(PYLADES *fades into background*)
    My Lord, this is the man from whom I took the chariot yesterday.
    I said you would make recompense. Telandros is his name.
ORESTES   Ah yes, thank you, my friend, and so I shall make recompense.
    You may have heard that the Leader of the Men met with a sorry accident

And now lies dead. From the several chariots he possessed
You may take one that pleases you.
TELANDROS   Thank you, my Lord. That is a noble gift for such a little service;
Your generosity is sure sign of the true Achaen blood.
I know, for my father...
ORESTES   Yes?
TELANDROS   Well, it is not a thing to boast about in Argos;
At least, till now.
ORESTES   Speak up!
TELANDROS   Well, my father fought for Menelaus.
ORESTES   You should be proud of that!
But... are you another judged as dead, as was the limping one?
TELANDROS   No, my Lord. I had nothing to claim and nothing to lose.
ORESTES (*to* TROPHONIUS)   By the way, friend, I do not think I have been fair to you.
Yesterday, you returned to me some objects I had lost – remember?
TROPHONIUS (*cautiously*)   Er, yes.
ORESTES   It so happens that the Lawgates had some pretty things like that,
We found them when we catalogued his goods.
Here you are; they are now yours, and you and I are quits.
TROPHONIUS   Thank you, my Lord. You are most generous.
TELANDROS   I said he had Achaean blood!
I saw you at the contest, when you fought the other princes
Hoping to be consort. I could tell by the way you used your sword.
That's how my father taught me and my brothers;
Men's work – not this dainty Cretan stuff.
ORESTES   I must try a bout with you, my friend.
TELANDROS   Not with a sword, my Lord Orestes; I know my master.
But without a sword...
(*takes up wrestling stance*)
ORESTES   Ha! You're on! (*grapples*)

(*Enter* COUNCILLOR, STEWARD, LEADER OF THE GUARD, *etc., in a hurry and slight disarray*)
COUNCILLOR   This would be disgusting conduct in the servants' quarters
    But in the Throne Room –
    Stop it! Here is the Queen.
(ORESTES *breaks off bout*)
ORESTES   Later, my friend. I'll beat you yet!
(*Enter* HERMIONE, ELECTRA and LADIES, *again in some disarray*)
ORESTES   Greetings ...
HERMIONE (*cutting in*)   Orestes! This is terrible! Now the Lawgates slaughtered.
    First the Marshall; now poor Kerewos.
    And by the same small blade, they think.
    No! It could not have been the one you wear;
    You were with me all the time; so were your friends, I think.
COUNCILLOR   Let them be searched, my Lady!
HERMIONE   What? Argive citizens?
COUNCILLOR   That one at least is not. (*points to* PYLADES)
HERMIONE   Orestes?
ORESTES   My men are at your command, my Queen.
(HERMIONE *nods to* LEADER OF THE GUARD *who searches them*; PYLADES *first, but he transparently has no weapon, sword belt, sheath – only the leather wrist-guards with their bobble ornaments; then searches others.*)
LEADER OF THE GUARD   No, Nor you! Right!
    My Lady, nothing.
HERMIONE (*to* COUNCILLOR)   And now?
COUNCILLOR   The room they used last night.
(HERMIONE *looks at* ORESTES, *who shrugs amusedly*)
HERMIONE (*to* LEADER OF THE GUARD)   Send your men.
(LEADER OF THE GUARD *details off two men who exit*)
    (*to* COUNCILLOR) But why? Why should they be slain?
COUNCILLOR   As yet, I see no sense in it. As yet. (*awkward pause*)
    My Lady!
HERMIONE   Yes, my Councillor?

COUNCILLOR   My Lady! Despite the shadow on our minds, yet there is business for your attention.
HERMIONE   Oh, no! Must we?
COUNCILLOR   You should bestow your pleasure on a new Leader of the Men.
HERMIONE   So soon? It seems indecent somehow.
COUNCILLOR   We must assure the safety of your person.
ORESTES   My love, that is my job, keeping you from harm.
HERMIONE   Dear Orestes!
COUNCILLOR   Ah! And so he died!
HERMIONE (*to* COUNCILLOR)   You said ...
COUNCILLOR   There are ample precedents, my Lady, to guide our choice.
   Not, I fear, my Lord Orestes.
ELECTRA   Who better than a scion of the House of Atreus?
COUNCILLOR (*to* HERMIONE)   My Lady, shall I answer?
HERMIONE   As if it were my question.
COUNCILLOR   These are the precedents: firstly that the consort never shall be Leader of the Men ...
ORESTES   What are these precedents you talk about? What stands between me and my clear-cut right to keep the Queen from harm?
COUNCILLOR   Here are the precedents!
(*Takes tablet from his assistant and offers to* HERMIONE)
   My Lady, read!
HERMIONE (*scans tablet*)   Yes I know. I only hoped ... (*hands tablet to* ORESTES)
   It is as he says, Orestes.
(ORESTES *turns over tablet wonderingly*)
COUNCILLOR (*slyly*)   Read it, my Lord Orestes.
(*But it is clear that* ORESTES *has no conception of reading*)
   Read the precedents, my Lord.
   What does the tablet say?
(ORESTES *unconsciously puts tablet to his ear; then as if realising he is betraying himself, throws it down. It does not break.*)
COUNCILLOR (*picking up tablet, slyly*)   The precedents are not smashed so easily.

ORESTES   Witchcraft!
COUNCILLOR (*easily*)   I am no sorcerer; just the Keeper of the
    Precedents.
  But do you now agree, my Lord Orestes,
  That we must seek elsewhere for the successor to the post?
ORESTES   I do not know just how the trick was worked.
  But tricked I am.
  Where is your candidate?
COUNCILLOR   As the tablet said, my Lord. Did you not read?
  The Captain of the Palace Guard, of course.
(CAPTAIN OF THE GUARD *shifts uneasily*)
CAPTAIN OF THE GUARD   My Lord Orestes, if you prefer...
    I would not mind...
COUNCILLOR (*to* HERMIONE)   My Lady, we present for
    your approval
  A worthy man to lead the men, well-tried in your service.
(*Pushes* CAPTAIN OF THE GUARD *forward; he kneels*)
HERMIONE (*hieratically*)   See this man! Who speaks for him?
COUNCILLOR (*steps forward and places hand on the*
    CAPTAIN OF THE GUARD'*s left shoulder*)
  The voices of the past enshrined in the precedents
  Say 'This is the man'.
HERMIONE (*again*)   See this man! Who speaks for him?
(STEWARD *steps forward to other side*)
STEWARD (*but looking sideways at* Orestes *all the while*)   The
    customs of the past, set in the just administration of this city
  Say 'This is the man'.
HERMIONE   Who speaks against this man?
(*Eyes swivel to* ORESTES *but he is an outsider at a strange
ritual*)
  See the Leader of the Men!
(*Tension is over*, COUNCILLOR, STEWARD, *etc., congratulate
the new Lawgates who stays kneeling.*)
COUNCILLOR   My Lady!
HERMIONE   Speak, my Councillor.
COUNCILLOR   Thus say the precedents: that the wealth, goods
    and chattels pertaining to the rank of Lawgates
  Be now invested in this man, your servant.

ORESTES   What? What's this trickery?
HERMIONE (*to* ORESTES)   Hush, dear. We always say this.
ORESTES   But . . . the whole vast fortune that Kerewos possessed!
   Why give it all . . . ? Yesterday, he was a servant, a member of the guard.
   What has he done to earn this huge reward?
HERMIONE   My dear, this is no reward! This comes to him by virtue of his post!
ORESTES   But he is nothing!
COUNCILLOR   He is the Lawgates of Argos and while he lives enjoys the privileges and possessions,
   The lands, the farms, the herds, the horses – all the panoply
   Which marks him out from lesser men.
   The produce and the progeny are his, to use or sell at will.
   For the estate he is accountable, down to the last field,
   The last chariot, the last arm-band, the last ring.
   For, my Lord Orestes, all these things are inscribed upon our tablets
   Showing in some detail their position, or their fashioning
   So that, should some dispute arise on ownership, her Ladyship may say
   'This belongs' or 'That does not' –
   So, my Lord Orestes, you can be reassured, there is no room for – trickery.
HERMIONE   My dear, you are still angry! How else should matters be arranged?
ORESTES   My Queen, your customs still are strange to me.
HERMIONE   Surely the House of Atreus would do the same as us?
ORESTES   In my country, all land and wealth is gifted by the king
   And should the holder die, reverts unto the king once more
   To be gifted once again according to the wishes of the king.
COUNCILLOR   How interesting, these most unusual customs of a distant land.
HERMIONE   My Lady, it is as well we have no kings in Argos
   Or else our precedents would need revision.

(THALAMATAS *comes forward*)
THALAMATAS (*to* ORESTES)   Fare you well, my Lord. You
    have been most kind to one in need but – fare you well!
ORESTES   Why leave me now? What is this treachery?
THALAMATAS   Once I had a farm, and lost it. That was the
    law,
    And how I fought against the law!
    Maybe I later gained another farm, or maybe not,
    I am an old man and easily forget things told me not a day
      before.
    But that was not the law. So, farewell, my Lord,
    For I would rather be a 'have not' in the law than be a 'have'
      outside.
TELANDROS   The old fool rambles. Let him go!
ORESTES   Go, then, but go far and quickly!
(*Exit* THALAMATAS)
COUNCILLOR   My Lord Orestes, all this is hardly relevant!
    Or is it? You were telling us the customs of your native land.
    Achaia did you say?
ELECTRA   Of course Achaia, the homeland of the Atridae.
CAPTAIN OF THE GUARD (*still kneeling*)   My Lady!
HERMIONE   Oh dear! I had forgotten . . .
CAPTAIN OF THE GUARD   My Lady, I have a griping in my
    leg.
HERMIONE   Oh dear (*hieratically again but hurriedly*):   In
    you become invested all pertaining to your rank.
    Guard it in the Mother's name.
COUNCILLOR, STEWARD, etc   So be it written down.
(CAPTAIN OF THE GUARD *stands*)
HERMIONE (*to* ORESTES)   Dear Orestes, do not be angry.
    This is our way.
    Come here, my dear.
    You must not be jealous of the Lawgates
    For both of you protect me in your different ways.
    (*to* LAWGATES) You, as Leader of the Men, dispose the
      forces on the outer walls and gates of Argos,
    While you, Orestes dear, keep vigil by my side.
    Now show your friendship, not your enmity.

(LAWGATES *offers hand;* HERMIONE *takes* ORESTES's *wrist and places their hands together;* ORESTES *unconsciously takes up the wrestling stance again and then becomes aware of what he does*)
ORESTES   Ha!
  Forgive me, love, and you, my friend.
  My conduct can only be excused by the shock I had
  To find my long-held, unquestioned attitudes and customs
  Unknown and meaningless within your realm.
  But now, my love, I recognise my place within the scheme
    of things.
  As you say, The Lawgates now commands the walls and gates
  While I, leading the Palace Guard ...
COUNCILLOR   Hrrm!
ORESTES   ... keep the final ring of bronze ...
COUNCILLOR   Hrrm!
ORESTES   ... protecting you. What now, old man?
COUNCILLOR   The precedents, my Lord. Did you not read
    them?
ORESTES   Do you dare to hold a tile against my throat
  As if it were a sword? Pylades, open wide!
COUNCILLOR   I do not understand your foreign oaths,
  But do you not understand precedents?
  My Lord, if the consort may not be the Lawgates
  How can he be the Captain of the Guard, the Lawgates' due
    successor?
HERMIONE   Oh dear! It would be nice!
COUNCILLOR   You appreciate, my Lord, that there is nothing
    personal in this.
  No animosity persuades my mind to these decisions
    somewhat adverse to yourself.
  If ... though this is obviously unlikely in the circumstances
    ...
  But if I were to die tonight ...
HERMIONE   No! You should not say such things!
COUNCILLOR   But just supposing!
  The precedents survive! (*drops tablet, which again does not
    break*)

(*Re-enter the two men sent on search*)
  Ah! My Lady, may I ...
HERMIONE But surely ... (*indicates* LAWGATES)
COUNCILLOR Forgive me, my Lady. Of course.
(*All look at* LAWGATES *who stammers into his ritual*)
LAWGATES Er, advance! Now, hold!
  Report!
FIRST GUARD Our search accomplished. Nothing found!
COUNCILLOR Oh! No weapon?
(GUARD'*s eyes swivel to* COUNCILLOR *but do not answer*)
LAWGATES Oh yes! No weapon?
FIRST GUARD Nothing found, neither in the room nor in the
  passages
  Nor underneath nor near the window of the room.
LAWGATES Oh! Retire!
(*All look at each other*)
COUNCILLOR A small Parnassian blade.
ORESTES Like this! (*slaps sword*)
COUNCILLOR (*privately*) Then not like that.
LAWGATES That slays and ... vanishes!
  (*to* HERMIONE) My Lady! I think we waste our time in
   search for weapons made by man –
  These are the arrows of the Huntress, showering divine
   displeasure on our race.
HERMIONE Beyond the Corinth wall might be true, but who
   invokes the Huntress here in Apia?
(*She scans room; glance falls on* ORESTES *and* PYLADES, *and hesitates*)
  Princess Amber! A private word.
ELECTRA Madam?
HERMIONE (*to* ELECTRA) What is that oath – or is it prayer
   – my Lord Orestes uses in his rage? 'Something open
   wide'
ELECTRA 'Pylades' is a Northern word, my Lady,
  It means the gateway to the Underworld.
HERMIONE Did he speak it to the Marshall of the Gate?
ELECTRA He had cause for anger, cousin. First my whip
  And then the Marshall's dagger at his throat.

HERMIONE   I heard him – speak like that – to Kerewos
　　Not by his hand these two men died, for we ourselves
　　Are witnesses to his innocence.
　　But has he brought into our land some potent curse
　　Which, spoken so, hurls down the hearer to the Underworld.
　　How is it warded off, my cousin,
　　In Achaia?
ELECTRA   Not from Achaia, Lady. I mean . . .
HERMIONE   Not from Achaia? . . . (*seeing many things*)
　　Oh!
　　(*to* ORESTES) My Lord Orestes, within this land of Apia,
　　　the Mother rules.
　　All other deities and powers obey her will.
　　Through me She speaks; these are her words . . .
ORESTES   I will hear no witchcraft; cast no spells at me!
HERMIONE   Let the Gates of the Underworld stay shut!

ACT 3

SCENE: *Throne room at Mycenae.*

ELENA   These men had feathers where other men have hair.
ERIGONE   My Lady, please. The Councillors require your
   word.
ELENA   Do not be frightened, sister, they will not harm us.
   We are not there.
PERILAUS   My Lady, is it agreed?
ELENA (*to* ALETES)   Watch the north coast road for men who
   walk the Gulf at night
   Wet to their waists.
PERILAUS (*to* ALETES)   Is there any substance in her words,
   or is she lost again?
ALETES   She is lost in a strange world – not this, for every
   night
   As it has always been, patrols go out along the coastal roads.
   Strangers have landed, on a moonless night or covered by a
   storm
   But we have picked them up within a day or two.
   But they are all sorts – refugees from Thebes or labourers
   denied an entry permit at the wall –
   Quite ordinary – not the monsters which inhabit her queer
   world.
ELENA   Aletes? Why are there no patrols from Sicyon?
ALETES   There are, my Lady, there are!
ELENA   Oh, not you, I was not asking you, dear brother.
ALETES   You spoke my name.
ELENA   No, not us, we are dead.
   Oh, why does Aletes let them through?
ALETES   She speaks my name yet does not talk to me.
ERIGONE   It is not you – your baby boy perhaps.

ALETES   Not one year old!
ELENA   Erigone! Aletes's hands are tied. Lead my people home!
ERIGONE   Yes, my Lady, but your Councillors . . .
ELENA   I have no . . . Councillors?
   Ah, Perilaus, you were saying?
PERILAUS   That the rate levied on the villages be as last year . . .
ELENA   Agreed?
ALETES   } Agreed!
PERILAUS
ELENA   So be it.
NICOSTRATUS   Your words are written down and will be acted on.
ELENA (*to* ERIGONE)   Why are you crying, sister?
ERIGONE   With joy, my Lady, to have you back again.
ELENA (*gently*)   Do not cry for me, sister. Cry for those who do not understand.
   (*To* PERILAUS *and* ALETES) And the next for my attention?
NICOSTRATUS (*to* PERILAUS, *handing tablet*)   Enforcement warrant, if you please.
PERILAUS (*to* ELENA)   This, my Lady, is an application to enforce your judgement
   By one Aglaia, wife of a fisherman . . .
   Fisherman? Of Lerna? But that is in the Argive jurisdiction! Nicostratus! What is all this?
NICOSTRATUS   There was an appeal from a judgement by the Queen Hermione . . .
ALETES   There have been enough of them in recent years.
NICOSTRATUS   And once again the applicant succeeds.
PERILAUS   The law is clear enough. The Queen in Argos has either lost her Councillors
   Or else . . . er . . .
ELENA   Her mind? It is a privilege of Queens.
PERILAUS   My Lady, no, I pray you, I did not mean . . .
ELENA   The case in hand?
ALETES   Surely we of Mycenae do not enforce our judgements on appeals
   From other jurisdictions?

PERILAUS   No! It is for the Argive court to settle this.
    Non-suited, my Lady?
NICOSTRATUS   Er, Lord Perilaus...
PERILAUS   Mmm?
NICOSTRATUS   If you read on...
    There is no satisfaction to be had in Argos.
PERILAUS   Come, come! They had our judgement, did they
    not?
NICOSTRATUS   That I have verified.
PERILAUS   There is one law in this land, and, while there are
    Queens
    In Argos, Pylos, Elis and in Sicyon,
    Then to the High Queen in Mycenae should they look for
        guidance and uniformity
    Or else there would be chaos.
    Anyone within its boundaries can walk into a distant town
    And know at once his rights and obligations, and get fair
        dealings in the market place.
    Foreign merchants, making any port around our coasts
    Find the same dues and regulations...
ELENA   Aletes, brother, I am pulled again. There is a journey
    we must take!
    Do not be afraid for I will take you home...
ERIGONE (*to* PERILAUS)   Uncle, you must not worry her like
    this.
ALETES (*to* ELENA)   I am not afraid, my Lady...
    (*to* PERILAUS) Can we end the business for today?
ELENA   It is ended! Listen!
(GUARDS *driven in by* ORESTES *and his mob.* ALETES *draws, slips in and gets his sword point to* ORESTES'*s throat*)
MONITOR OF THE GUARD   Draw! Draw! Draw! Now mark!
ALETES   Hold. What is this?
ORESTES   Hold, my friends. We have arrived!
ALETES   What is this?
ORESTES   Well, this is a royal welcome with a pretty Cretan
    plaything at my throat!
    So this is Mycenean hospitality!
ALETES   Who are you, bursting in like this?

ORESTES   Will you rest? Take some wine? Wash off the dust of
    journeying?
        Oh no! A bronze blade tickling at my life.
        What is this? Who are you? I am welcomed better by the
        cottagers round Argos,
        Who have the decency to set a bench and jug before a
        wanderer
        Before they seek to learn his name and business.
ALETES (*to* GUARD)   Take his sword!
ORESTES   Steady, boys, he has my heart-beat on a needle-
    point.
ALETES   No matter what the cottagers in Argos do!
        Your name and business!
ORESTES   I am a reasonable man. Give me your name and
        business first and if I think you worthy of the confidence,
        I'll tell you mine.
ALETES   Aletes, Lawgates of Mycenae. Now speak.
ORESTES   Well, well, the man of war himself.
        And how is business in your territory?
        Hold! I am the Consort of the Queen in Argos.
ALETES   Who comes with swords into the Palace of Mycenae?
        I need a better tale than that.
ORESTES   Why not, when acting escort to my Queen?
        Do you not do the same?
ALETES   The Queen Hermione, coming here?
ORESTES   Not while you block the way, my dancing boy.
        No doubt it is the custom in this land to keep a Queen
        Awaiting in your corridors. We have more decency in Argos.
ALETES   Produce your Queen.
ORESTES   Hermione, Queen in Argos, forward please.
(HERMIONE *pushes through*)
PERILAUS   It is Hermione. My Lady, welcome to Mycenae.
HERMIONE   Ah, Lord Perilaus, now you're the one I've really
        come to see.
ALETES (*leaving* ORESTES)   Guard, in two ranks, on the end
        men, wheel!
        Guard, alert. To the Royal ... salute!
HERMIONE   Greetings, Aletes. How is your little boy?

ORESTES   Well, that was neat! Do that again!
ALETES (*to* ORESTES)   I beg your pardon? (to HERMIONE)
　　Madam, he is well.
ORESTES   That... dancing thing your boys performed.
ALETES   Madam, we were not expecting you or else you
　　would have met
　　Our welcome at the city gates.
ORESTES   We met a sort of welcome – but not for long.
　　So this is Mycenae they all talk about.
HERMIONE   Lord Perilaus here must surely have expected me
　　(*to* PERILAUS) Do you think that you can treat me like a
　　naughty child
　　And think me weak enough to sulk in Argos?
PERILAUS   Me?
ORESTES   That's it, my love, you tell him.
ALETES   Madam, before we come to business, do you think
　　perhaps the courtesies could be observed?
ORESTES   Listen, my friend, if you are fretful of the way I
　　point your failing manners
　　Quarrel with me, not with my woman.
ALETES   Behave yourself; you are in the presence of the
　　Mother.
ORESTES   What, her?
HERMIONE   Hush, dear. (*advances and curtsies to* ELENA)
　　Greetings, Mother on Earth...
　　(*to* ERIGONE) Is she with us?
ERIGONE   I do not know.
NICOSTRATUS (*to* HERMIONE)   Hullo.
HERMIONE   Why, Nico, I did not see you there! How are you,
　　now?
NICOSTRATUS   Fine... but... what's all this?
ORESTES (*to* ALETES, *indicating* ELENA)   Is she in a
　　trance?
ALETES   Be quiet.
ORESTES (*to* HERMIONE)   Who have we here?
HERMIONE   My brother, Nico.
ORESTES   Your brother? You never told me you had a brother.
NICOSTRATUS   Several.

ORESTES   Several? Sons of Menelaus?
HERMIONE   Of course. What surprises you?
ORESTES   What ... are you? What are you doing here?
NICOSTRATUS   Court writer. Assistant to Lord Perilaus.
ORESTES   What? A son of Menelaus scratching clay.
   What are the others? Kitchen hands?
NICOSTRATUS   No, not kitchen hands. One works in bronze
   in Pylos
   Another ...
ALETES   Please, this is not seemly in the presence of the
   Queen.
ORESTES   But here be wonders! Sons of Menelaus, King that
   helped to pull down Troy
   And here his children, not kings or even princes
   But ... servants. Hermione, my sweet, why do you rule in
   Argos
   When you have brothers who might occupy the throne?
PERILAUS   You are not in your highlands now, O Northerner.
ORESTES (*to* NICOSTRATUS)   Are you content with this?
NICOSTRATUS   I am happy here.
ORESTES   Well, that's one less problem which I might have
   had to face.
HERMIONE   What about my problems. Perilaus, undermining
   my authority in Argos?
ALETES (*to* HERMIONE)   Madam, would you adjourn to the
   guest room, please.
   This is not seemly in the presence of our Queen.
ORESTES (*to* ALETES)   But is she present? This ... apparition
   (*indicating* ELENA) here ...
ALETES   Mind your words. She is my sister.
ORESTES   Well, your sister, then, was asked if ... she
   (*indicating* ELENA) was with us. She didn't know. Do
   you?
ALETES   Queenship is everywhere, throughout our land,
   throughout our history.
ORESTES   I would prefer a portion of it here and now.
NICOSTRATUS (*to* PYLADES *who is poking among his tablets*)
   Leave them alone!

ALETES   Amidst this turmoil? Clear those people from the room
   Even your own Queen's voice is lost amidst this din.
HERMIONE   Yes, would you, please?
ORESTES   All right, my lads. Quiet, you miserable crew!
   We have done well enough. Now get yourselves some sustenance.
   Drinks on Mycenae!
   Not you, Pylades. Stay around; I have a need for you.
ALETES   Monitor of the Guard! Take up your posts once more.
MONITOR OF THE GUARD   From the tail! Form Column! Go!
ORESTES (*to no-one in particular*)   I have observed your pretty Cretan ways
   But whereas you play games of 'Draw' and 'Mark' and 'Thrust'
   With dancing boys, I work with men.
HERMIONE (*turning from* PERILAUS *to* ORESTES)   My dear, I think I've made my point.
PERILAUS   It is a voluntary convention, entered into freely by each queendom throughout Apia.
   No-one can hold you to it if you wish to make your own way through the legal woods.
ORESTES   Thank you for nothing. If there stands a precedent between us and the way we choose
   We hack it down.
PERILAUS   And when your term is done, another consort hacks your laws to bits.
   A sorry plight, to be a litigant in Argos.
ORESTES   My time! That precedent went first!
(*Silence*)
PERILAUS (*to* HERMIONE)   Am I to understand the term of office of the Argive consort
   Now is perpetual?
HERMIONE   Why not? Am I not Queen in Argos?
   Can I not make my own laws as I please?
PERILAUS   Did not your Councillors advise against . . .
ORESTES   What Councillors?

PERILAUS   Why the Keeper of the Precedents, the Lawgates ...
ORESTES   The Keeper of the Precedents was enamoured of his
   little cakes of clay
   Yet Pylades here, this oaf, carousing round the Palace after
   dark
   Spills his wine in the Archive Room ...
PYLADES   I drunk it first.
ORESTES   Quiet, you Minyan toad! ... And all the precedents
   go back to mud.
   The Keeper – quite heartbroken – died of grief.
   Or something. Anyway, he died.
   It hardly seemed worth while appointing anybody else.
   If anybody doubts our ruling, and imagines up a precedent,
   We send him to Pylades. After all, he is the one who last
   Made reference to the tablets.
ALETES   And the Lawgates of Argos, how did he die?
ORESTES   Ah, you are ahead of me. Yes, he died, a sorry
   accident.
   He was a nice lad, but far too trusting for the job.
   One day we had a friendly trial of strength.
   I broke his neck.
ALETES   Queen Hermione, may I speak?
HERMIONE   Proceed.
ALETES   You have, with good reason to your mind, spoken of
   interference
   From us here in Mycenae in the affairs of the Argive state.
   May I seem to interfere once more.
ORESTES   Be careful, lad.
HERMIONE   We will hear him.
ALETES   If it is your will that the posts of authority in the realm
   of Argos
   Be not filled, and that power falls where it may,
   So be it. I would have nothing else to say.
HERMIONE   It is my choice, my decision.
ORESTES   Suppose it were not, my friend, what then?
HERMIONE   You may speak, Aletes.
ALETES (*to* ORESTES)   If there were compulsion on a Queen
   to act against her will

>Then the whole confederation would be at the service of that Queen
>To set things right.

ORESTES   Yes, I thought it might.

HERMIONE   It is my choice. My father did not need a Leader of Men
>When he ruled Argos. He was the leader.

PERILAUS (*dry laugh*)   Precisely. When the Queen Elena left her realm for Troy
>You became the Queen, but in your infancy, your father was the Leader of the Men.

HERMIONE   He was King! Just as Orestes now is King.
>Even when young, I did not like to see my consorts
>Have to run or die when once they served their time.
>Now I feel the years upon me and would keep the man I have.

ORESTES   Thank you, my love.
>Will you now confirm that Argos has the right to go its own way
>As and when it pleases?

PERILAUS   Confirmed.

ALETES   Confirmed.

ORESTES   And no more tribute payable?

ALETES   Tribute? From Argos?

PERILAUS   Do you refer to the annual offering to Mother-on-Earth?

ORESTES   Offering, gifts, call it what you like. I call it tribute.

PERILAUS   It is at your choosing, to honour the Goddess as you will.

ORESTES   We will make our offerings in Argos.

PERILAUS   As you will.

ORESTES (*to* HERMIONE)   We've done it, love! Now, homewards bound.
>(*to* PERILAUS *and* ALETES) And that, I think, concludes our business for today.

(*Enter* ELECTRA)

ELECTRA   My business now begins.

ALETES   Who is this?

ORESTES How did you get past the guards? You were to stay
    outside.
ELECTRA Your mountain goats are running wild
    And goat-like seek to mount the Palace maids.
    The guards are busy herding them, while maidens, such as I,
    Are led to safety.
ALETES: Who is this?
ELECTRA: I do not need to ask your name, Aletes.
    Nor yours, Erigone. Nor yours, Elena, Mother-on-Earth
    (*to* ORESTES) Look at them, the Aegisthidae, gasping,
    Not recognising one who shared the same womb with them.
PERILAUS Electra!
ALETES Greetings, sister. It is a long time since we met.
ERIGONE Greetings, sister.
ELECTRA I will not be greeted as sister by the products of
    adultery
    For Agamemnon was my sire.
PERILAUS Now I come to think of it, there is, I think, a ban on
    you
    From entering this city.
ORESTES Think again; she is my guest.
PERILAUS It may have lapsed, of course.
ORESTES Of course. But as it happens, we were going
    anyway.
ELECTRA Not I, while shame sits on the throne of Atreus.
ORESTES Steady, now! Let us consolidate what we have won
    And pick our future quarrels when the time is ripe.
ELECTRA This is a past and present quarrel that struck my
    father dead
    And put this booby on the throne.
ALETES (*to* HERMIONE) Would the Queen Hermione join us
    for a meal before she leaves
    With her – attendants?
ELECTRA Look at her! If she had been a peasant's brat
    Would she not have been left out on the mountainside?
    Would you breed Queens from her?
ALETES Be quiet! Get out!
ELECTRA You tell me, Aletes, to be gone?

I have the blood of Atreus pulsating in my veins
And so has Queen Hermione; and Nicostratus here.
Orestes here is more a brother to my mind than all of you
And any one of us can make a better claim upon that throne.
Get out, you say. Get out, Aegisthidae!
(*She drags* ELENA *from throne and throws her centre front.*)
ALETES *comes towards* ELECTRA *and* ELENA *and, as he crosses* PYLADES, PYLADES *stabs him and he falls, reaching out for* ELENA)
ALETES   Elena! Mother! (*dies*)
(ERIGONE *runs forward to* ALETES *and crouches by him, weeping*)
NICOSTRATUS (*to* ELECTRA)   Curse you, curse you, for laying hands upon the Queen.
(PYLADES *grabs him*)
HERMIONE   He is my brother, mind what you do!
  Why did you have to do a thing like that to poor Aletes?
PYLADES   I dunno. I didn't think I'd get another chance.
NICOSTRATUS   Let go! Let go! The Queen has fallen!
ORESTES (*to himself*)   Too soon, Pylades, just a mite too soon. Ah well, no option now.
NICOSTRATUS   Guard! (PYLADES *puts hand over his mouth*)
HERMIONE   No!
ORESTES   Mind what you do, Pylades. Mind what you do!
  (*to* PERILAUS) And you, old man, will you shout and die?
  (*goes to door and listens, relaxes and comes back*)
ELECTRA (*mounting throne*)   Agamemnon, you are revenged.
ORESTES   My men still keep them occupied.
  I could have wished a better disposition,
  My goats this side of the fence, the guards outside,
  Before the challenge made. Now what to do?
ELECTRA   Avenged. Avenged.
HERMIONE   Back to Argos. We have no business here.
ORESTES   Electra will not come. Do I leave her to the mob?
HERMIONE   She is mad. Mad as Elena here.
ORESTES   All or nothing, love. Add Mycenae to your crown.
HERMIONE   Are you mad too? Can you fight Mycenae on your own?

ORESTES   If we leave now, we will not reach safety in the
    Argive territory
  Before those dancing boys come racing at our heels.
  If we stay, here at the centre of Mycenae, perhaps we can
    inhibit action
  With these two (*indicates* ELENA *and* ERIGONE) as our
    hostages.
ELECTRA   Or like King Atreus, who was placed by Zeus upon
    this throne
  And set to rule this land ...
PERILAUS   No! That's blasphemy!
ORESTES   Keep still, old man, and think on this:-
  Are you worth more alive to me than dead?
  (*to* HERMIONE) Can you not bend your brother to your
    side
  For I would prefer Pylades unencumbered.
HERMIONE   I can try.
  Nicostratus! Can you not be loyal unto our common blood
  If I should take the Mycenean crown?
ORESTES (*to* PYLADES)   Let him speak.
NICOSTRATUS   I serve the Queen!
  No! Guard! (PYLADES *clamps down*)
ORESTES   This is the worst madness of the lot.
  A son of Menelaus, one who might be king himself
  Would rather be a servant to a child without a mind.
HERMIONE (*to* NICOSTRATUS)   Nicostratus! Will you let us
    take our leave
  And call this ... trouble ... just an accident?
ORESTES (*to* PYLADES)   Do not let him speak again, I read
    the answer in his eyes.
  (*to Hermione*)   All or nothing, love!
HERMIONE   What will you do with her? (*points to* ELENA)
ORESTES   I do not know. (*kneels by* ELENA *to look more
    closely*)
  How can a thing like this command the minds of men?
ELECTRA   Or like King Agamemnon, he who pulled down
    Troy. Avenged at last.
(ELENA *lifts one hand and points at* HERMIONE)

ORESTES   I will have no spells cast, no prophesies!
ELENA   It is a boy, Hermione.
ORESTES   What is? Hermione?
PYLADES   She got a bun in the oven!
ORESTES   Hermione?
HERMIONE   It seemed too soon to tell.
   I have been barren all these years; as consorts came and
      went.
   I thought I did not have the spring of life within myself.
   Oh, I have heard the women's chatter from behind the screen
   But how was I to know this welling up for what it was.
PYLADES   You rung the bell, Orestes!
ORESTES   A boy! A boy!
   No 'boy' is not enough. Let us give this prince a name!
ELECTRA   Name him 'Vengeance'.
ELENA   He has no name.
HERMIONE   Oh no! Not still-born, let him live!
ORESTES   Would you cast a spell on him?
   This sword cuts spells and those that speak them.
ELENA   He will live long.
ORESTES   That's better. Now I shall give him a name!
ELENA   Whatever you give him, name, rank, lands or power
   He shall lose.
ORESTES   No spells, I said! (*strikes*)
   No prophecies! (*strikes again*) No curses on my son! (*kicks
      the body*)
ERIGONE   Not that! She was a Queen!
ORESTES   She prophesied against my son.
ELECTRA   Death to the Aegisthidae!
   Father, you are avenged.
PYLADES   There's still another one.
ORESTES (*to* ERIGONE)   Now you! Prophesy your life away.
ERIGONE   Mother, what is your will of me? (*rises*)
   (*to* ORESTES)   This is my prophecy, that you will die
      before I do.
ORESTES   Ha! That one I can disprove, right now!
ERIGONE   It is as valid as 'It is a boy'.
ELECTRA   Death to the last Aegisthidae!

HERMIONE   No, no more blood! I feel unwell.
ORESTES   Steady, love. Come, sit here.
   You there, (*to* ERIGONE) attend my Queen!
   'It is a boy' shall be as valid as your span of life.
(PERILAUS *on one knee by* ELENA)
HERMIONE (*to* ERIGONE) Cousin, this was not premeditated.
ERIGONE   Yet Elena knew! She knew.
ORESTES (*to* PERILAUS)   I have upset your tidy world and trampled on your principles
   And in the new world I must make there is no room for memories,
   Nor yet for witnesses.
   No man shall point at me and say 'He killed the Queen',
   For pointing fingers turn to swords, when there are enough of them.
PERILAUS   There is a precedent.
ORESTES   I know, but I will not be hunted through your streets by a screaming mob.
   Precedents like that are best forgotten
   And those that call them up are best destroyed.
   Now, old man, will you die quietly by your Queen?
ELECTRA   There will be no more Queens!
PERILAUS   Your guest, who, uninvited, occupies the throne
   If only as a temporary resting place
   Now indicates there will be no more Queens.
   Kill me or let me live, but a screaming mob would hunt you through the streets for that.
   Put your Queen Hermione on that throne and
   No matter what the reality of her power, you may have peace.
ORESTES   You are an easy traitor to the spirit of your precedents.
   What is the reality in this show of sweet submission?
PERILAUS   I now would talk awhile with Nicostratus, here.
   Then I will go as quietly as you wish, if you still wish.
ORESTES   You think if you could quieten him
   It might persuade me to a better value of yourself?
   You may be right, but do not be too long
   You may be wrong.

PERILAUS (*to* NICOSTRATUS)   Mycenae's Queen is dead;
   her brother too.
   I may be next, but even if this Prince should let me live
   I would have very little profit from the span that's left to
      me.
   Who will be Keeper of the Memories when I am gone?
   This man Pylades, here?
   Who will be Lawgates? My maybe executioner?
   Who will be Priestess after young Erigone? No doubt
      Electra.
   Who will be Queen? (*his gesture encompasses both*
      HERMIONE *and* ERIGONE)
   The Moon that was is in a cloud
   That being rent by mountain winds might only show
   The ending line that started with Andromeda.
ORESTES   What is this southern baby-talk?
   Use words that men can understand.
PERILAUS (*to* NICOSTRATUS)   I will ask Pylades to be good
      enough to free your mouth
   Your upraised voice could dissipate the cloud,
   Your silence adds another Mother to the song.
   Pylades, let him go.
ORESTES   I do not understand your words, old man.
   I have a deep mistrust of spells and secret words
   But if your incantations do not call up silence
   I have a magic in this bronze that does.
   Pylades, let him go.
(NICOSTRATUS *rubs his mouth but says nothing*)
ORESTES   Your incantations work! Let their effect last long!
NICOSTRATUS (*sullenly*)   I will not shout.
   He stinks of mule.
PERILAUS   With your permission, Lord Orestes, I will have
      the bodies moved
   To a more appropriate place.
   May I call the servants?
ORESTES   You die if you raise your voice.
PERILAUS   Will you stay all night with them?
   And your lady, too?

ORESTES   What's in there (*pointing to opposite side from where they entered*)
PERILAUS   The entrance to the royal suite.
ORESTES   Pylades, look around. (PYLADES *exits*)
ELECTRA   Throw their bodies out for the crows to feed upon. Are we to give ceremonial burial to the foul Aegisthidae? Was not my father butchered for their benefit?
HERMIONE   Please! No more talk of things I would forget.
ORESTES   Please, Electra.
PYLADES (*re-enters*)   Not a mouse.
ORESTES (*to* PERILAUS)   You may remove them by yourselves. Return at once.
(PERILAUS *and* NICOSTRATUS *carry off* ELENA *with as much dignity as they can*).
   (*to* PYLADES)   And him.
(PYLADES *drags off* ALETES *by one foot. Comes back shepherding* PERILAUS *and* NICOSTRATUS)
ELECTRA   How satisfying the crimson puddles on the floor;
   Yet only two. Orestes, dear,
   Please add a third and make my vengeance whole.
(HERMIONE *screams*)
ORESTES (*to* ELECTRA)   Quiet!
   (*to* PYLADES, PERILAUS *and* NICOSTRATUS)   Can you clean this up?
(ELECTRA *comes down from throne, takes off her cloak and lovingly soaks up the blood*)
ORESTES   Pylades, if I ever did I have need of you!
PYLADES   Oh good. Which one?(*draws sword*)
ORESTES   That will encumber you (*takes sword*)
   Escort Princess Electra to the royal suite
   And lead her mind up happier paths.
PYLADES   I can do that, and more.
   You got a three month's start; but yet I'll catch you up. (*exits with* ELECTRA)
(ORESTES *goes to* HERMIONE *and leads her to the throne*)
ORESTES   It is done, my love. Now rest, High Queen of Mycenae,
   Mother of my son-to-be.

    (*to* PERILAUS)   Can you, in a voice that has no overtones, call a servant
Order wine and nourishment, and keep alive?
PERILAUS   I can, my Lord. (*goes to entrance; sounds gong and waits.*)

CURTAIN

HED'S TALE

I'm pretty sure I was invited to this party in error. In fact, it makes a lot of sense if the fellow I had been chatting up at the party – no, the first party, I mean – had been a vet. You know how it is at parties – groups form, dissolve, coalesce and divide without the need for anyone to say 'Do you know?', 'This is', 'Have you met?' and so on.

Still, perhaps they did, for that would explain why I was holding forth to this fellow on animals in opera; not just the wolfhounds brought on to add colour to the 'Don Carlos' hunting scene or the mule to pull the cart on for Canio or Dulcamara, but real imaginative stuff such as strapping wings on race-horses and lowering them on slings with Brunnhilde and Co. Up. It was at about this point that this other fellow took me by the elbow and said something about being time to go on to the other party as agreed. I couldn't actually remember agreeing anything of the sort but the chance of a bit of fresh air between drinks seemed a good thing and might well have dispersed the highly illegal breeding programme I was evolving for a race of Fafners for future productions of Siegfried.

It was an older house we went to, and the main room which housed the party did just that without decanting the surplus into the hall and halfway up the stairs.

My first impression was that it wasn't my sort of party at all and this at once struck me as odd because all parties were my sort of party. This isn't bragging, it's just that in my job people who know what I am don't invite me that much so I make the most of those I do get to. But, generally, one can size up a party at a glance – sporty, arty, sexy or just plain boozy, yet this one seemed to have no common factor but was made up of one of everything.

There was quite a large crowd, with a lot of coming and going, and I dare say that with a bit more fresh air between my drinks I would have realised what was special about their coming and going. The fellow I came with wasn't much company and though he seemed to know everyone did not bother to introduce me – but I've said something like that before, haven't I – parties are like that these days. Groups form, dissolve, coalesce and divide, don't they? Like hell they don't, not at this party.

My acquaintance was making small talk with some city type

when this girl appeared at my right elbow. Let us now consider the nature of words and the conventions of those who put words to paper.

That last phrase of mine ought, in normal circles, to convey the idea that this girl walked, weaved or otherwise insinuated herself through the surrounding throng approaching at three miles per hour finishing somewhat right of centre to my vision. Dear normal circles, I am not using conventions. I was looking at, indeed admiring my right elbow when 'ping' there she was. Out of thin air, as they say, though I make no allegations or accusations regarding the thinness or thickness of the air at the party. And please don't say I was too sozzled or tired or engrossed to have seen her coming. Apart from the fact that I have to keep my eyes open in my job, I'm a fellow who can – oh dear, bragging again. Anyway, let us say it is unusual for me to overlook the approach of the opposite sex. Right? And what is more, she was talking to this city type, obviously in the middle of some girlish anecdote, with him listening and making the appropriate noises as if she had been there all the time. It is possible that my professional mask of Oriental inscrutability slipped somewhat, as my first acquaintance (what was he, anyway? Accountant, insurance man?) felt it behoven to explain, 'Denise, cashier in the garage upstairs.' Explain! Not a word such as 'It's all done by mirrors' or 'We're a witches' coven, you know', the sort of thing to reassure a fellow. And what garage upstairs? I could believe there might be an office, employment bureau, gambling den or brothel upstairs but not a garage on the first floor of an early Victorian house in a Pimlico square.

I had decided I did not want any more to drink and put my half-empty glass down on a passing tray. Sorry, I'm talking conventionally now; the tray was being carried by a cocky little fellow with 'ex-jockey barman' written all over him; life was hectic enough with materialising females without adding self-levitating trays to the entertainment. I found I could retreat slightly from these characters I was with and prop myself against the wall by the door so I could analyse the situation. Question one: was I drunk and suffering from some aberration of vision – an enlargement of the blind spot so that chunks of the room came and went as I turned my head? Answer one (a): no, I only drink to be in the mood for what's going and never so as to be unfit for future developments, if you see what I mean. Answer one (b), no, because when I was admiring my right elbow I could see the carpet beyond and a nice pair of ankles – oh, that's why I was admiring my right elbow – and Denise was instantaneously in the centre of my field of vision.

Question two: was I dead and was this a sophisticated Hell? Answer two: not having been dead before, I couldn't tell if the routine tests of pinching oneself had any relevance. So I might be. No, all I had to do was walk out of the door, out into the street and back to the original party where they would tell me when I died and what of. If. So I walked out of the door, into the street and there was Pimlico all right and a bus going past but it was raining so I thought I'd go back. Well, I wanted to know just what they did at witches' covens, and if there was a garage on the first floor, how they got the cars up the stairs. Anyway, professionally speaking, I should know about the garage as I was certain it wasn't on my books. Same room, same party, more or less. A few folk I'm pretty sure weren't there before; definitely no jockey-barman.

Then suddenly 'ping', the fairy fell off the Christmas tree! There, in the centre of the room, where the lights enhanced each other, where there was space, she was. Young, tall, fair, slender, innocent, untouched, desirable, with eyes of cornflower blue – the impressions flowed over me in succession – and lost, as if she, like me, was seeing the room for the first time. She seemed to know everyone in a hesitant, shy sort of way and suddenly and strongly I sensed that everyone knew her, respected her, almost depended on her.

The atmosphere in the room felt as if a lot of well-mannered people were aware of royalty in their midst and, not wanting to intrude, were waiting to be spoken to, smiling encouragingly as if to say 'We are here if you want us', yet at the same time waiting for a lead. I realised then that the room was crowded. Everyone I had seen there before was there, including the ex-jockey, and whoever had been missing before had arrived with Cornflower. Their private conversations still murmured round the edge of the room, but there was this tension, this awareness of Cornflower everywhere. Especially for me. I realised I was still in the 'Denise, city gent, first acquaintance' group and I spoke to Denise for the first time.

'I know you and I haven't been introduced, but,' nodding at Cornflower, 'can you introduce me?'

I know that sort of thing isn't done at parties these days but this was special. She was apart.

Denise looked at me blankly, then at Cornflower, and then, shortly, 'Don't be silly! How can you possibly meet her? You've never met her.' Now that's what I like about these people, their explanations are so simple, reasonable and utterly impossible. Well, if I couldn't meet her, as I'd never met her, then the sooner I met her, the sooner I would meet her. So, squad, 'shun, by the right quick march, as you bloody well were, she's gone again. Ping! What is more, the crowd was thinner as if quite a few others had pinged with her. I retreated to the wall, baffled, and Denise and co. were once more in my vision. The tension had gone out of the room, and Denise was giggling.

'I expect she went to the loo,' someone said and her companions had that look of enjoying a funny but dangerous joke. There was the same feeling all round the room but clearly the 'she' referred to was not Cornflower; there had been too much respect for her for that sort of talk.

Right, I certainly wasn't drunk and I probably wasn't dead, unless Number 24 buses run through Hell on their way to Golders Green, so what was my problem?

It was the garage upstairs that fretted me more than the disappearing trick and as I focused on this problem I found a likely answer. Either the house must be on different levels front and back, which was unlikely from my impression of Pimlico geography, or it backed on to a multi-storey car park with garage facilities, and that was quite likely even though I couldn't quite place onto what street it might front. With this easing of the mind came a possible solution to the disappearing trick. This was a scientific/industrial/financing type of party demonstrating holographs, 3-D projections that is. I felt normal, except that my longing to see Cornflower was neither scientific nor industrial nor financial. If my theory was right, however, the state of the art was far more advanced than I had thought, and anyway, if Denise, for example, was really upstairs but projected downstairs, how could her holographic image carry on a conversation with me? Now if my image were projected upstairs to talk to the real Denise simultaneously, did that eliminate or double the problems of communication? No, leave that one. Now to prove my theory, ladies and gentlemen, I will now pass my hand through Denise – Christ, no, I had better not! They did these holograph things with lasers and my hand would probably drop off. I looked round at the party again. You crafty lot, you're all in this and I'm the outsider, the guinea-pig to be observed and sniggered over. And sure enough, there was a handy-looking type giving me a big grin, coming across the room towards me with another, slightly worried-looking, bloke. It was Worried who spoke and put me back to Square One.

'Oh hullo, you're the new vet, I understand. I run Maggs Farm upstairs and I have to meet you soon to discuss my winter feed problem. What cattle nuts can you recommend?'

I've gone mad, I thought, stark, staring, bonkers. I had adjusted myself to accepting a first-floor garage in Pimlico but I was not standing for any bloody herd of cows on the second floor. And who said I was a vet? Yet clearly Nut-case wanted an answer and repeated, as if rehearsing a script, 'What cattle nuts can you recommend?' and all I could say was 'Whitworth or B.S.F', which was quite smart considering, though Nut-case just looked blank.

Anyway, his companion saw the joke in a big way and I thought he would hurt himself and there I was in bright sunshine in a wide, quiet, street in an obviously country town, up against a Land Rover smelling of manure and there was Worried Nut-case in a corduroy jacket, leaning over to the off-side to speak to me.

'Hello, you're the new vet, I understand. I'm Maggs from Burrside Farm; well met. I have some troubles you might help on. I've a winter feed problem with my Herefords. Cake doesn't seem to suit them and I wonder what nuts you might recommend.'

I realised that the Land Rover was at a petrol pump under the arch of the entrance to an old coaching inn, and there was this handy-looking type, in dungarees now, on the end of the pump filling her up and grinning at me and there, over his shoulder in a little glass box set in the wall, was Denise at the telephone and blast me if there wasn't that wretched jockey in a parody of a page boy's uniform loitering under the portico of the 'Stofferley Arms', by a notice 'Stoner's Garage at rear'.

'What cattle nuts can you recommend?' came the voice again and all I could bloody well say was 'Whitworth or B.S.F.'. Maggs just looked blank but my friend on the pump curled up laughing and put half a gallon of three star in his right boot before he could control himself. May I always have an audience like that for my merry quips.

It seemed incumbent on me to say something as everyone else seemed speechless; the responsibility for breaking the warm silence riled me so that I positively snarled, 'Where the hell am I – Ambridge?' But no, I was in the Pimlico house once more with Maggs gaping at me, Stoner checked in mid-laugh, Denise just beyond him, turning from the city gent towards me, and the jockey nearly dropping his tray. The other guests were giving typical reactions to someone's faux-pas and, when the city gent murmured in my ear, 'That was rather bad form, old boy', I realised it was mine. I also realised we had a full house again and that Cornflower stood in her pool of light so lost and alone and infinitely beautiful as before. But only for a few seconds and she was gone again.

'That's got rid of Ambridge,' muttered someone behind me and then Cornflower flicked into view for a second and was away once more. Her laser needed a new battery, I thought, and then realised my rationalisation was no longer valid. We had all been wearing different clothes 'upstairs', if that's where that warm, quiet, street lay: certainly I had never in my life owned a suit of clothes or a tie such as I had been wearing. They might be doing clever things these days with lasers but they haven't trained the damn things to act the instant valet yet. It's a film set, of course, and this party a type-casters' jamboree – hadn't I been subconsciously referring to 'types' and 'characters' without seeing the reality of their staginess? No, that won't do – the make-up and wardrobe boys and girls couldn't move that fast – the unions wouldn't allow it. The back projections too – I could have sworn that warm, quiet street stretched for a quarter of a mile in the sun, dipped through a copse and disappeared round a hill a mile or so off – there had been no join between set and back-cloth, and once again you can't fit a mile of road into a first-floor room in Pimlico. Or second-floor either, for that matter. I didn't want that explanation to be right either as Cornflower would cease to be real and only be everyone's fairy doll, everyone's fairy-tale princess, everyone's dream bird. I wanted her to be herself, not a typed actress.

More lasers on the blink, with people flicking on and off and a sense of alarm building up in the room. Then it steadied and the only absentees seemed to be Denise and Stoner. Farmer Maggs had recovered his wits but still seemed put out with me. 'They told me you were a vet,' he said accusingly.

'What? Me, a cow's midwife?'

'What are you then?'

Here comes the point at which I lose friends and aggravate people, where otherwise attractive girls walk, weave or otherwise insinuate themselves away into the surrounding throngs at four miles per hour. But I'm proud of my job and if this mob gives me the cold shoulder they can stick their lasers where James Bond nearly got stuck. 'I'm an Income Tax Inspector.'

Surprise, surprise, he laughed. A ripple of good humour ran round the room, a friendly interest, a pleasurable anticipation. I *am* mad, that proves it. Only my first acquaintance, he of the original invitation, looked taken amiss, in fact definitely poorly but he said nothing. 'Ping' – Denise and Stoner amongst the 'also present'.

'I've explained the joke to Denise and she's leaving it in,' Stoner announced with glee.

Pirandello – characters in search of an author, Rosencrantz and Whatsisname are dead, that's the situation and there was Maggs glaring at me out of his Land Rover with Stoner cawing and shaking petrol off his boot and Denise giggling in her goldfish bowl and Maggs saying, accusingly, 'You're no vet.'

'What, me a cow's midwife?'

'What are you, then?'

'I'm an Income Tax Inspector,' and that blew the fuses if ever anything did! Full house on the ground floor, lying around and laughing their silly heads off and Cornflower, not sure of the joke, in her crowded solitude.

I had two lines of thought going on more or less simultaneously; this Stofferley place was ringing a little bell now – it was either a television serial, a visual Ambridge, a British Peyton Place or a magazine serial, but more likely the former though I'm not a box-watcher myself. Drawn from life, it was advertised, and that was just about it. I was being drawn into, or written into somebody else's – yes, the 'she' they just referred to – into her story whether I liked it or not. What's the betting Cornflower is the 'narrator' because no one else is ever 'upstairs' when Cornflower is downstairs. And she was so lost because she had so little time to live her own life.

Thought number two – if I can walk out into the rain into Pimlico once more, then next time I'm going with Cornflower on my arm and we're not coming back. If. Perhaps I really couldn't have left, perhaps I was on a string and could be let out like my original acquaintance was in order to recruit a new character and must inevitably be drawn back. What chance then of getting the 'narrator' even out of the room? This is where I start trying, even if I have to serve notice on her under Section 51, Taxes Management Act 1970, to have her present her pink form at my office for my inspection. (Old departmental joke!) As I moved towards her, I realised that everyone was cocking their ears ceiling-wards, but I heard no more sound than of a chair being pushed backwards. This struck me as odd as I hadn't heard Maggs drive up in his Land Rover. Twit, there isn't any Land Rover up there, it's just a story but, in that moment, I realised that for these people it had become their life, not just a story, and you don't need to put strings on people who don't want to run away and I might get like that. After all, District Inspector of Taxes for Stofferley must be higher up the ladder than second deputy in Pimlico.

A couple more 'excuse mes' and 'do you minds' and I was up there in the pool of light and looking into those incredible blue eyes and finding nothing more to say than 'Hello.' I'm not certain she heard me for though I happily ignored the quiet click of a door upstairs and a soft footfall on the landing, it was clear that Cornflower, and everyone else for that matter, had heard it and knew what to expect. There was straightening of seams and neckties and the jockey was fiercely wiping his tray where he had slopped something earlier and glaring at me as it were my fault. Well, you can't go on saying 'hello' to a girl who looks rather apprehensively over your shoulder, and as I turned I picked up the quiet footsteps on the stairs and realised that She, the life-sucker, Countess Dracula in person, was going to pay us a visit. This would be the woman I had to get Cornflower and myself away from and I suppose I was bracing myself to meet the bug-eyed Medusa from outer space. The reality was laughably different: a middle-aged female on the short side, in a knitted brown dress, shapeless I was going to say, but a regular cylinder isn't exactly shapeless. Brown carpet-slippers, brown hair, a good forehead and surprisingly gentle eyes. She came diffidently through a path cleared by the congregation towards Cornflower and me, with not a sign that she owned all present, not necessarily excluding me.

'Hello, Jennifer,' she said to Cornflower in a nice quiet voice. Jennifer. Jennifer's Diary. No, that was a society gossip column, but someone had nicknamed the Stofferley saga that. Jennifer the virgin, often in peril of rape, seductions and similar male pleasantries but always avoiding such traps without even being aware of her danger.

Jennifer responded, so I nip in smartly 'Hello, Jennifer' and, sure enough, I get a shy hesitant smile and if I let myself get written into the script I reckoned I knew enough to get that shy, hesitant smile on my shoulder next morning. Dammit, no, how does one fight ping!

This could be a torment, a real Hell, and I recalled a film I had seen that had Don Giovanni in Hell, perpetually on the point of success when, ping, he went back to the beginning again. That's Hell!

Then, She was saying to Jennifer, 'Aren't you going to introduce me to your new friend?' and I thought, silly bitch, how can she meet me if she's never met me, but Jennifer was saying, in a voice that was music to my ears:

'Oh, Miss Lamont, this is the new tax inspector, Mr Wilkins.'

'No,' I said, 'the name's Hedley, Hed to my friends, Big to my enemies.'

'Pleased to meet you, Mr Wilkins,' said She, and then to Jennifer, 'I didn't know we had a tax office in Stofferley.'

'No,' said Jennifer in beautiful cadences, 'we've just opened one.'

It shook me to hear such blasphemies on that sweet tongue and, horrified, I burst in, 'Only the Board of Inland Revenue can open tax offices, but I knew at once it was a mistake. If Stofferley needed a new vet, someone was sent out to get a new vet, and if Stofferley needed the Board of Inland Revenue, then someone would be sent out to get the Board of Inland Revenue, and guess who, and me only a second deputy and not even in boot-licking distance of the men who lick the boots of the boot-lickers by letter – patent to the Commissioners, the Board of Inland Revenue. But, I thought, She might get her strings on this mob and she had a finger-hold on me, but if there was one grim bunch of characters she'd never get so much as a cobweb on, it would be the Board. Ah, Board, to the rescue, tarra-tarra!

Now, I didn't go ping, of course, I couldn't with both Her and Jennifer downstairs but I had my own private little vision, a parody of Stofferley, if you like.

The hot sun beat down on the rutted street and on the grim file of horsemen coming easily with leathers creaking, their Stetsons over their eyes and their Colts slung low on their thighs, and at their head a dour man with a silver star on his breast. The townsfolk ran before them and clustered protectively outside the Stofferley Saloon. (Hitch horses at the rear.) The dour man addresses them; 'You all know me, Sheriff Johnson from Paper City. Well now, there's some counterfeit code numbers being passed in the bars down there and Ah here tell y'all got yourselves an illicit tax office up in these yar hills. Ah sent ma deputy Hedley upalong to see it right and he ain't come back. So Ah'm just gonna tear this two-bit two apart 'til Ah find Hedley and burn down that lil' ole counterfeit office of your'n.'

'Johnson!'

'Yes, Mr Johnson, suh,' said one of the posse.

Johnson, frisk 'em and the man or woman with a wrong code number on 'em will dance on air afore sundown. And you, Johnson, give Johnson a hand there.'

'Sure, Mr Johnson, boss.' (This Johnson business is another Departmental joke but I haven't time to explain it here.)

I realised She was speaking to me again, with a quiet, almost apologetic little smile on her face. 'I don't think we need bother with too many technicalities that would only interest the specialist. We'll assume that all the necessary formalities have been properly completed.'

I had a quick look at my private vision, and the posse had bowler hats on, and were filing quietly into the Stofferley Arms for a quick sherry before leaving Hedley, in the best traditions of the Department, to solve his own problems.

Well, that was one thing I had learned, no, two! I had – indeed all of us characters had – the power to disrupt the proceedings to some extent and, in fact, I had done so three times, firstly with my nuts and bolts gag, then with my Ambridge faux-pas, and then by not being a vet. To some extent these were permissible, even desirable, in that the story unfolded in an unexpected way, but the second thing I had learned was that I did not seem to have the power to modify Stofferley out of recognition. It had been with Her too long, she knew every stone, every bit of the lives of her characters, and I had little chance of fighting her on her own ground. But She was speaking to Jennifer about me.

'Do you think he would be a comfort to the bank manager's widow?'

Jennifer looked both puzzled and shocked. 'Mr French! I didn't know he had died.'

'Yes dear, he's going to have a heart attack in his office.'

'Oh, poor Mr French, he's been very kind to me.'

'Yes, my dear, and I'm sure Mr Wilkins will be most sympathetic to Mrs French in her distress.' She turned to me. 'By the way, Mr Wilkins, perhaps you would tell Jennifer why Mrs French would seek your assistance.'

I looked wildly round the room. Who was I supposed to get shacked with? I spotted Mr French first – I should have guessed – my first acquaintance who had been sent out to get a vet and had boobed – and he was white as a sheet. Then I realised I was being coolly appraised by an elegant female somewhat older than myself and twice as experienced, and by the way she was being fussed over by that military gent I could see a nice little triangle being written in for me. But this is ridiculous, it's Cornflower I want and I'm not going to be fobbed off with Mr French's cast-off, relict and sole beneficiary.

'Mr Wilkins.' I was brought back to realise that She had asked me a question, and I didn't have time to put together a considered answer. 'Oh, she's after his Enhanced Pension rights.' This wasn't the best of answers but it apparently pleased Her and was acceptable to Jennifer.

'Goodbye, Mr Wilkins, so nice to have made your acquaintance,' and she was padding off upstairs.

Hell, I must get back to my office quick – but quick – and instruct my counter clerk to deal with all Enhanced Pension rights queries himself. No, stop, that won't do, I've already found out I can't beat Her on Her own territory. There was the distant sound of a door shutting and a chair scraping and ... ping! My beautiful Cornflower had left me. So, in rapid succession went Mr French, a young couple (bank assistants?), a broad-shouldered Johnny (policeman?), a professional gent (doctor?), a couple of nobodies (ambulance men?), and there was Mr French with us again. But this time, everybody was making sure they did not see him – he had been written out – and he looked as lost as Cornflower had first seemed to me. He looked at me pitifully and I shrugged; what could I do? He gave one last look at the elegant Mrs French and I thought, he really loved that woman, and then he went to the door quietly and into the hall and out of the front door on to the shiny wet streets of Pimlico. And presumably went home to his missus and kids, but what was the time scale to all this? Had he only just been round the corner for a paper or would he find, like the Flying Dutchman, they are old and pale and their sweethearts are dead? I realised I was sweating, for in a few seconds I'd be sitting in my new office with the counter-clerk sticking his head round the door and saying, 'Would you see Mrs French, please, sir? She has an Enhanced Pension rights query I can't handle.'

I had to stop this with something quite different, something as strong as the Stofferley saga but which couldn't be grafted on to Her story, something which would bring Cornflower downstairs once more so I could grab her and run like mad before She caught hold of the strings again. Something with a power and continuity of its own, that would for a moment divert her from the chase, a golden apple for Atalanta. Troy! That was it. I'm bragging in a subdued way now but I did once try my hand at a blank verse rehash of the Troy story in the light of Professor Blegen's work and the Linear B decipherment. Ping! I was in a fine sunny office with pale yellow walls and a set of mahogany furniture in the true Ministry of Works tradition but no, immediately I imposed on them the milk-white walls of Troy, the great bronze gates of Ilium.

> I spat the sand from my mouth
> And set to scramble from the dust-dry ditch
> Where your javelin shaft had sent me.
> And there you were, Petreus, grinning your foolish grin
> Your face on the edge of the ditch.
> But, oh, Petreus,
> There was a Phrygian arrow in your throat
> And many men lay dying in the dust.
> How my head ached, Petreus, but at least I lived.
> But where in the swirling mists was Troy
> And where my friends?
> Had I been left for dead – our enterprise thrown back?
> Or did we still advance?
> And then it came to me
> If I were the last of all the Greeks alive
> Yet would I advance.
> Then as the mists rolled on, a man in purple tunic
> Stood my way – a Phrygian archer
> From their outer posts.
> Yet as I crouched within my shield
> And groped the blood-stained dust
> For the spear I had before I fell
> So did he slowly crumble to the ground
> And I could see the venting gash within his back.
> Where some Argive spear had caught him as he ran.
> So I was not alone!

I paused for breath and the milk-white walls were slowly stained to works yellow and the bronze gates turned mahogany. Oh no you don't, I thought savagely, you've got three more bloody acts of this to listen to.

I breasted the mist as a swimmer in the foam
And there, there was the golden helm of Menelaus
There were my comrades with their flashing spears
That threw back to the sun the first fine rays of dawn,
There were the shining towers,
There were the brazen gates,
There were the milk-white walls of Troy ...
I saw the Trojan princes shield to shield
And step by step withdraw within the lofty gates.
I saw the gates swing shut.
And then some madness spoke to me and said,
'You will never storm the gates of Troy
But at least there is a tale
That you can tell your children
And their children, too
"I have laid hands on Troy!"'
And I raced ahead and placed my hands
On the cold white walls and cried,
'I have you, Troy!'
But a rain of stones from the well-manned tower
Then beat me down
A bronze spear sliced my leg and but for bold Antiocles
Who with his shield bestrode me as I crawled away ...
I cannot leap or run as I once did
Yet with my stout spear in my hand
No one shall pass me where I stand.

And there we were again in the lower room, Cornflower by my side and everyone else looking somewhat dazed, if not frightened, as any bunch of Stofferley citizens might feel after being ambushed by a company of Phrygian archers. I turned to Cornflower and said urgently, 'Jennifer, my love, my love, come with me now.'

She smiled, the first really, truly smile I had seen on her face and she moved slightly towards me and then checked puzzled. 'I'm caught up, somewhere. Mr Wilkins? Can you please...' But, of course, there was nothing there, nothing I could see or cut or break or undo. She was just caught, that was all. I was caught, too, because I heard the door upstairs slam and feet on the stairs, more dominant than before, and there She was in the doorway.

She advanced into the room and the crowd fell back as before, but She only gave me a hard look and passed with set mouth. The crowd parted for her and she squatted by a bookcase I hadn't seen before. Running her finger along the shelves, She picked out three volumes and headed back upstairs, studiously ignoring me. Homer, Euripides and Sophocles, I bet my boots; she was going to fight me on my own ground. But, you old spider, I bet you haven't got Dares the Phrygian and his 'Little Troy'! I'll beat you yet. Let me see, she'll try tracking down my lines, assuming them to be Euripides or Sophocles (now you know why they call me Big!) so that she can put the play on at Stofferley Town Hall. She might still let the Tax Inspector produce it, a nice unexpected touch, but She couldn't have her characters going round selling tickets for 'You know, that Troy thing by whatsisname'. I toyed with the idea that a world premiere of 'Seek the Fair Helen' would suit me fine, even in Stofferley Town Hall, but no, I'd settle only for Cornflower first, Cornflower last and another neglected masterpiece mouldering in my bureau in the real world. I turned to my heart's wish. 'Jennifer, Jennifer, my love. Have you a coat, it's raining.' Jennifer smiled.

'Raining. I'd forgotten rain.'

I bet that blasted sun always shone in Stofferley.

'No, I have no coat.'

I pulled gently at her arm but clearly it hurt her; she was still held. 'I can't, Mr Wilkins, I can't move.'

No, she couldn't, not while Madame Spider Lamont held her firmly fixed in her mind's eye in Stofferley. Then I noticed the crowd; a slackening of tension, almost an eroding of personality, becoming ordinary, rather than larger than life, and I knew that good old Homer had entered into Spider's mind, filling it with the clash of bronze on the windy plains by the wine-dark sea. For a little while the spell was broken and I knew Cornflower was mine. I also knew as if it had been shouted at me that just as my name wasn't Wilkins, hers wasn't Jennifer. Unbelievably, so improbably, this was my moment of truth, when all the dials on the fruit machine of my life read 'Win' and I knew her name. 'Helen,' I whispered, and she half ran, half fell into my arms. I spun her round and let her momentum take us to the door and into the hall and then a fine rain was falling out of the dark on our up-turned faces.

I knew it was not the end of the battle for though the cords might run idly through an inattentive hand, there would come a time when even Hector could not keep back the serried ranks of Stofferley and the cord would tighten again to draw my Cornflower away from me.

I had half an hour for certain, perhaps an hour and I knew what had to be done though, in all conscience, it was not the sort of thing I'd want to rush in other circumstances. My pad was too far away and the precious time would be wasted in travel, so that meant it had to be one of those bed and breakfast places round Victoria Station where no-one queries the absence of baggage and eyebrows are only raised if you're both still there for breakfast. Again, not my style at all, but what else?

* * *

She lay on my arm, her golden hair streamed across my shoulder and those incredible blue eyes lay hidden by the translucent lids. I've beaten Her, I thought; you can pull your cord marked 'Jennifer the Virgin', innocent and undefiled, and she may even go back to you, but you can't use her any more, she's no use to you now.

Tomorrow, I thought, I must begin the most important and final courtship of my life. I didn't know how long she had been out of this world, and I must bring her back gradually and gently, show her the treasures that Stofferley couldn't have: the opera, the ballet, the galleries and museums, even a ride on a Number 24 bus, if you like. Tomorrow, I must show you my world, handling you with all the care I am capable of, working gently towards the next night we will spend together, on our honeymoon. The lashes flickered and those incredible blue eyes looked up at me and smiled. That's tomorrow, I thought firmly, tonight's different and this time she came to me knowing what she wanted and glorying in the discovery of her womanhood.

You can't use her any more, she's no use to you, she's no longer Jennifer the Virgin but Helen the Woman. You'll have to write her out and if you write out the narrator, the story's finished.